WHAT CAN I DO NOW?

WHAT CAN I DO NOW?

Preparing for a Career in Radio & TV

EAST CHICAGO PUBLIC LIBRARY
EAST CHICAGO, INDIANA

Ferguson Publishing Company, Chicago, Illinois

Copyright ©1998 by Ferguson Publishing Company, Chicago, Illinois

All Rights Reserved. This book may not be duplicated in any way without the express permission of the publisher, except in the form of brief excerpts or quotations for the purpose of review. The information contained herein is for the personal use of the reader and may not be incorporated in any commercial programs, other books, databases, or any kind of software without the written consent of the publisher. Making copies of this book or any portion for any purpose other than your own is a violation of United States copyright laws.

Printed in the United States of America
V-4

Library of Congress Cataloging-in-Publication Data

Preparing for a career in radio & TV
    p. cm. -- (What can I do now?)
    Includes bibliographical references and index.
    Summary: Focuses on what to do now to prepare for a career in broadcasting, while also presenting information on specific kinds of work in radio and television.
    ISBN 0-89434-250-9
    1. Broadcasting--Vocational guidance--Juvenile literature. [1. Broadcasting--Vocational guidance. 2. Vocational guidance.] I. J. G. Ferguson Publishing Company. II. Series
    PN1990.55.P74   1998
    384.54'023--dc21   98-18446
                                                CIP
                                                AC

Ferguson Publishing Company
200 West Madison, Suite 300
Chicago, Illinois 60606
800-306-9941
www.fergpubco.com

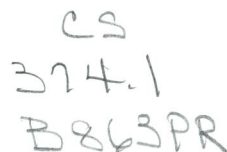

About the Staff

- Holli Cosgrove, *Editorial Director*
- Andrew Morkes, *Editor*
- Veronica Melnyk, *Assistant Editor*
- Veronica Melnyk, Beth Oakes, Tim Schaffert, Elizabeth Taggart, *Writers*
- Connie Rockman, MLS; Alan Wieder, Bibliographers
- Patricia Murray, Bonnie Needham, *Proofreaders*
- Joe Grossmann, *Interior Design*
- Parameter Design, *Cover Design*

Contents

INTRODUCTION	ix

SECTION 1: RADIO & TV

WHAT DO I NEED TO KNOW?	3

SECTION 2: CAREERS

BROADCAST ENGINEER	19
RADIO PRODUCERS AND DISC JOCKEYS	29
RADIO AND TELEVISION ANCHORS	39
REPORTERS AND CORRESPONDENTS	49
SCREENWRITER	59
SPORTSCASTER	69
TELEVISION DIRECTOR	77
TELEVISION PRODUCER	87
WEATHER FORECASTER	97

SECTION 3: WHAT CAN I DO RIGHT NOW?

GET INVOLVED	109
DO IT YOURSELF	129
SURF THE WEB	135
READ A BOOK	143
ASK FOR MONEY	151
LOOK TO THE PROS	163
INDEX	167

Introduction

If you are considering a career in radio or television—which is presumably the reason you're reading this book—you must realize that the better informed you are from the start, the better your chances of having a successful, satisfying career.

There is absolutely no reason to wait until you get out of high school to "get serious" about a career. That doesn't mean you have to make a firm, undying commitment right now. Indeed, one of the biggest fears most people face at some point (sometimes more than once) is choosing the right career. Frankly, many people don't "choose" at all. They take a job because they need one, and all of a sudden ten years have gone by and they wonder why they're stuck doing something they hate. Don't be one of those people! You have the opportunity right now—while you're still in high school and still relatively unencumbered with major adult responsibilities—to explore, to experience, to try out a work path. Or several paths if you're one of those overachieving types. Wouldn't you really rather find out sooner than later that you're not cut out to be a news anchor after all, that you'd actually prefer to be a broadcast engineer? Or a producer? Or a reporter?

There are many ways to explore the radio and television industries. What we've tried to do in this book is give you an idea of some of your options. The section "What Do I Need to Know about Radio and Television?" will give you an overview of the field—a little history, where it's at today, and promises of the future, as well as a breakdown of its structure (how it's organized) and a glimpse of some of its many career options.

The "Careers" section includes nine chapters, each describing in detail a specific radio or television specialty: broadcast engineer, radio producers and disc jockeys, radio and television anchors, reporters and correspondents, screenwriters, sportscasters, television directors, television producers, and weather forecasters. The educational requirements for these specialties range from high school diploma to M.A. These chapters rely heavily on first-hand accounts from real people on the job. They'll tell you what skills you need, what personal qualities you have to have, what the ups and downs of the jobs are. You'll also find out about educational requirements—including specific high school and college classes—advancement possibilities, related jobs, salary ranges, and the future outlook.

The real meat of the book is in the section called "What Can I Do Right Now?" This is where you get busy and DO SOMETHING. The chapter "Get Involved" will clue you in on the obvious, such as volunteering and interning, and the not-so-obvious: summer camps and summer college study, volunteer opportunities, and professional broadcasting organizations that welcome student members.

In keeping with the secondary theme of this book (for those of you who still don't get it, the primary theme is "You can do something now"), the chapter "Do It Yourself" urges you to take charge and start your own programs and activities where none exist—school, community, or the entire nation. Why not?

While we think the best way to explore radio and television is to jump right in and start doing it, there are plenty of other ways to get into the broadcasting mind-set. "Surf the Web" offers you a short annotated list of radio and television Web sites where you can explore everything from job listings (start getting an idea of what employers are looking for now) to educational and certification requirements to on-the-job accounts.

"Read a Book" is an annotated bibliography of books (some new, some old) and periodicals. If you're even remotely considering a career in broadcasting, reading a few books and checking out a few magazines is the easiest thing you can do. Don't stop with our list. Ask your librarian to point you to more radio and television materials. Keep reading!

"Ask for Money" is a sampling of radio and television scholarships. You need to be familiar with these because you're going to need money for school. You have to actively pursue scholarships; no one is going to come up to you in the hall one day and present you with a check because you're such a wonderful student. Applying for scholarships is work. It takes effort. And it must be done right and often a year in advance of when you need the money.

"Look to the Pros" is the final chapter. It's a list of professional organizations that you can turn to for more information about accredited schools, education requirements, career descriptions, salary information, job listings, scholarships, and much more. Once you become a college student, you'll be able to join many of these. Time after time, professionals say that membership and active participation in a professional organization is one of the best ways to network (make valuable contacts) and gain recognition in your field.

High school can be a lot of fun. There are dances and football games; maybe you're in band or play a sport. Great! Maybe you hate school and are just biding your time until you graduate. Too bad. Whoever you are take a minute and try to imagine your life five years from now. Ten years from now. Where will you be? What will you be doing? Whether you realize it or not, how you choose to spend your time now—studying, playing, watching TV, working at a fast food restaurant, hanging out, whatever—will have an impact on your future. Take a look at how you're spending your time now and ask yourself, "Where is this getting me?" If you can't come up with an answer, it's probably "nowhere." The choice is yours. No one is going to take you by the hand and lead you in the "right" direction. It's up to you. It's your life. You can do something about it right now!

Section 1

What Do I Need to Know About

Radio & TV

So, why'd you pick up this book?

Are you a sports fan, interested in a career that will allow you to watch basketball games for a living? Or maybe you're a music fan, and you're anxious to skip to the chapters on radio producers and disc jockeys. Or maybe traveling the world is more your speed, and you're hoping to read "How to become a reporter in ten easy steps." Though this book doesn't outline anything as simple as ten easy steps to success, it will introduce you to people working as producers, sportscasters, writers, and others involved in putting together the thousands of programs aired on radio and TV across the country on any given day. And though there are some tales of overnight success in the broadcast industry, you won't read of too many of them in this book. These are people who have worked hard in the highly competitive radio and TV industry—not in the pursuit of fame or wealth, but because they love the work.

GENERAL INFORMATION

In the movie "Contact," scientists receive a transmission from intelligent life on another planet. This transmission doesn't feature some scaly alien saying "Greetings, Earthlings"; it is a transmission originally from our own planet, from the opening ceremony of the 1936 Berlin Olympics. At first startled and upset by the appearance of Adolf Hitler on the monitor conducting the ceremonies, the scientists eventually determine that the message is actually a friendly one. "By sending back that broadcast," Jodie Foster's scientist assures everyone, "they're saying 'We heard you.' " This scene demonstrates the significance of the sounds and images broadcast around the world for the last several decades, and the role that radio and television has played in our lives. The scene also shows us the power of a single image, or a single voice.

General Information, continued

For centuries, people have desired to send their messages quickly around the world. The twentieth century, with its broadcast technology, has been influenced by this desire unlike any other time in history. The power and mystery of the radio broadcast has been evidenced by a number of events: In 1938, Orson Welles' (1915–1985) live radio broadcast of "The War of the Worlds" was so realistic with its simulated news coverage, that many Americans sought refuge from a Martian invasion; the radio-transmitted voices of Tokyo Rose (b. Iva d'Aquino, 1916–) and Axis Sally (b. Mildred Gillars, 1901–1988) were used as emotional warfare during World War II to disturb American soldiers with taunts about the girlfriends and wives they left behind; and Franklin D. Roosevelt's (1882–1945) fireside chats, for the first time, brought a U.S. president's voice and spirit close to the public he served.

Instantaneous worldwide communication had first become a reality in 1895 when an Italian engineer, Guglielmo Marconi (1874–1937), demonstrated how to send communication signals without the use of wires. In the early 1900s, transmitting and receiving devices were relatively simple, and hundreds of amateurs constructed transmitters and receivers on their own and experimented with radio. Ships were rapidly equipped with radios so they could communicate with each other and with shore bases while at sea. In 1906, human voice was transmitted for the first time by Reginald A. Fessenden (1866–1932). Small radio shows started in 1910; in 1920, two commercial radio stations went on the air, and by 1921, a dozen local stations were broadcasting. The first network radio broadcast (more than one station sharing a broadcast) was of the 1922 World Series. By 1926, stations across the country were linked together to form the National Broadcasting Company (NBC). Four years later, the first radio broadcast was made around the world.

Though the advent of television changed the kind of programming available on the radio (from comedy, drama, and news programs to radio's current schedule of music, phone-in talk shows, and news updates), there has been a steady growth in the number of radio stations in the United States. The United States alone has more than twelve thousand radio stations. However, until the government lifted restrictions in the mid-1990s, allowing companies to own more stations in one market, some radio stations suffered because of a smaller audience, and therefore, less advertising revenue. With larger broadcast companies continuing to buy up smaller companies, the radio industry should survive as cost-effective competition against TV and the Internet.

Modern television developed from experiments with electricity and vacuum tubes in the mid-1800s, but it was not until 1939, when President

Fast Fact

The percentage of U.S. homes with at least one TV receiver: 98. The percentage of people who get their news primarily from TV: 70.

Franklin D. Roosevelt used television to open the New York World's Fair, that the public realized the power of television as a means of communication. Several stations went on the air shortly after this demonstration and successfully televised professional baseball games, college football games, and the Republican and Democratic conventions of 1940. The onset of World War II limited the further development of television until after the war was over.

Since television's strength is the immediacy with which it can present information, news programs became the foundation of regular programming. "Meet the Press" premiered in 1947, followed by nightly newscasts in 1948. People who bought early TV sets just for the novelty of it, or to gather everyone around the tiny, snowy screen to see a favorite niece sing on a locally broadcast talent show, were soon rewarded by the rapid expansion of the industry in the 1950s. The Federal Communications Commission lifted a freeze on the processing of station applications, and the number of commercial stations grew steadily, from 120 in 1953 to the 1,540 broadcasting television stations of 1996.

It was in the 1960s that television's power became most apparent: together the country mourned the death of President Kennedy; witnessed the murder of his alleged assassin, Lee Harvey Oswald, by Jack Rub;, and formed opinions on the Vietnam War based on live TV news footage. The successes and failures of NASA programs brought viewers together, from the first steps on the moon, to the famous, near-fatal mission of Apollo 13; from the first space shuttle launch, to the tragic explosion of the Challenger. And Princess Diana's life and death were documented in thousands of images, including the worldwide broadcast of her fairy-tale wedding, and her funeral, which drew a record number of television viewers—2.5 billion people.

But the big three networks (NBC, ABC, and CBS), which, along with PBS, reigned for many years as primary sources of information and entertainment for millions of people in the United States, have consistently lost viewers to cable, satellite TV, the Internet, and video rentals. This hasn't stopped new networks, such as FOX, UPN, and WB, from developing and competing. And although more and more people are looking to the World Wide Web as a source of information, it could be years before the Internet develops into a reliable, trustworthy source of news and of quality entertainment, with the reach of TV and radio.

STRUCTURE OF THE INDUSTRY

Keep track of the number of hours you and your family spend in front of the TV and compare it to the national average—seven hours a day for each household. With so much time spent watching television and listening to the radio, a person can learn a lot about the structure and history of broadcasting; no wonder so many people pursue work in sports, news, screenwriting, and other broadcasting careers. In any given hour, a cable or satellite viewer may have a choice of one hundred programs; this number is increasing as more specialized cable channels develop original programming. And as we channel-surf with ease, sitting back with our remote controls, thousands of people are hard at work to bring us these programs. Over three hundred thousand people are employed in various ways by radio and television, both on the local and national level. Commercial radio employs about half, and commercial television about one-third of the total. The others are employed by broadcasting headquarters, including network offices and public broadcasting stations.

Some people in radio and TV, such as disc jockeys, talk show hosts, news anchors, and sportscasters, are prominent around the nation, or their local community, their voices and faces familiar to large audiences. Others work behind the scenes, putting together the many programs aired on radio, public TV, and cable on any given day. There are also engineers maintaining the broadcast equipment and salespeople selling airtime to advertisers to keep the station profitable. In television, large stations located in metropolitan centers can employ several hundred people, whereas a small station in a small city may employ as few as thirty-five people. In radio, the smallest station may employ only four or five full-time people. And some programs are put together by people working on a freelance basis—producers, directors, and writers employed by a station or a production company from project to project.

> *"Over three hundred thousand people are employed in various ways by radio and television, both on the local and national level."*

Obviously, your local Fox channel doesn't have the resources to put together an episode of "The X-Files." So how does the show manage to find its way piped into your home by a local station? Many television and radio stations are affiliated with one of the national networks (such as FOX, ABC, CBS, and NBC). An affiliate station is not owned by the network, but merely has a business contract; the network then supplies the affiliate station with a large amount of programming. "The X-Files," along with most of the original comedies, dramas, and news magazines in prime-time television are supplied by the networks; the affiliate stations put together local daily news broadcasts, coverage of local sporting events, and specials of regional interest.

> ## Trials of the Century
> The trial of O. J. Simpson, which dominated TV news for months, was not the first to be dubbed "The Trial of the Century" by the press—in 1935, Bruno Hauptmann, accused of murdering the infant son of Charles Lindbergh, also received "The Trial of the Century." This earlier trial, which attracted over seven hundred news people, is considered the event that brought radio news of age.

Ever been frustrated by the sudden cancellation of a favorite TV show? Or maybe the radio talk show you listened to every morning was suddenly replaced by a music program. Well, you may have been the only fan of these programs; ratings systems determine what people are watching, what radio stations they're listening to, and when. Maybe you've even served as a Nielsen family, filling out a diary, listing the programs you watched during a specific week. With numbers compiled by Nielsen ratings surveys, networks and affiliates determine what to charge advertisers for airtime during their programs. The highest-rated programs don't always have the highest ad rates, however; the Nielsen surveys also provide numbers about the *kind* of audience (such as young or old, women or men) watching a specific program, and some advertisers prefer to target specific age groups and genders. Because commercial radio and TV stations rely on advertising revenue to stay successful, much in the broadcasting industry (scheduling, staff, salaries) is determined by ratings.

Cable television networks operate under some of the same arrangements as commercial television stations. Some cable networks are advertiser-supported. Although one cable station may seem to rely entirely on reruns of "M*A*S*H," "The Love Boat," and other old, commercial-television product, others create their own programs. Cable networks that focus on specific subjects of interest, such as the Travel Channel and FoodTV, create special programming for their audiences. Other cable networks (such as HBO and Showtime) are subscriber-supported, and run motion pictures, sports or entertainment events, and movies produced specifically for cable.

Even the worst program on TV takes up its fair share of space in the air as it's transmitted along electromagnetic waves. So, as an attempt to keep things in order in a variety of ways, there is the Federal Communications Commission (FCC). Congress established the 1927 Federal Radio Commission,

The Industry, continued

which in 1934 became the FCC. The FCC is involved in many aspects of broadcasting, from business matters to the content of programs. The FCC supervises and allocates air space, makes channel assignments, and licenses radio and television stations to applicants who are legally, technically, and financially qualified.

The commission also sets limits on the number of broadcasting stations that a single individual or organization can control. These limits were relaxed, however, in the mid-1980s—broadcasters today no longer must perform as many public affairs and public service functions, the license renewal process is easier, ownership requirements are more lax, and it takes less time to buy and sell a station. In 1992, FCC regulations were relaxed even more, so a single company could own up to six stations in one city and sixty stations nationwide. Previously, an owner was limited to one AM and one FM station per city, and twelve nationwide. This new leniency has paved the way for large station and network mergers in recent years. The Telecommunications Act of 1996 created even more leniency, allowing phone companies to enter wider cable markets; this is expected to result in heavier competition among cable companies for the TV viewer.

Careers

In what other industry could you have a career playing your favorite music all day, or giving the play-by-play of a baseball game, or organizing the day's newsworthy events into a broadcast with the power to influence thousands, maybe millions, of people? Of course, not all jobs in the broadcast industry are ideal—some involve a great deal of stress at low salaries; and many broadcasts, even on the national level, only reach small audiences. In many small stations, jobs may be combined; an announcer may shoot news film, a secretary may write copy, an on-the-air sportscaster may serve as a salesperson.

Though some people achieve great wealth and fame in radio and TV, others seek out less competitive positions within the industry and settle into them. A sports lover, uninterested in working her way up into a position with a network sports department, may make a living as a camera operator for a local station; a radio disc jockey may prefer to work in a small town where he has more control over the play list than he would in a larger station.

TV sitcoms, news broadcasts, radio talk shows—all involve the collaboration of a number of professionals from the initial planning stages to the actual broadcast of the final product. Many of these professionals can work in both radio and television, while other careers are industry-specific. You will also discover that there are many more off-air careers than there are of the on-air variety—so don't tune out opportunities as a supporting player in these fields:

Off-Air Careers

Management. The job of *general manager* requires a unique combination of business ability and creativity. General managers are almost always people who have had successful experience in sales, programming, or engineering. Their responsibilities include the handling of the daily problems of station operations in consultation with program managers, sales managers, and chief engineers. They determine the general policies for the station's operations and supervise the execution of those policies. They normally handle the station's relations with the FCC and other government bodies and participate in many community activities on behalf of the station.

Program directors plan a program schedule and integrate programs to give the station a broad audience appeal. The program director of a station, in collaboration with the general manager, determines and administers the station's programming policies and plans the most effective program schedule for the station. He or she works with the producers and directors (who plan and supervise the production of programs, both in rehearsal and during broadcast), on-air personalities, and other members of the department in developing new programs or improving old ones.

The traffic department is little understood but serves a vital function in a broadcasting station. It is the heart of the station's administrative operations, through which all instructions regarding programming and sales must be cleared. The department maintains the logs of the station's daily program activities, which are used by the programming, sales, and accounting departments. This job is generally the responsibility of a *traffic manager,* who may be assisted by one or more traffic clerks.

Preproduction, Production, and Postproduction. Preproduction consists of the planning and organization it takes to get a radio or television show up and running. A radio or television show must be scripted, budgeted, and scheduled in order for it to be a broadcast. Actors and actresses must be hired, and props, sets, and costumes must be prepared. Production consists of the actual shooting of the television show or newscast, and in radio, the broadcasting of the show. Postproduction consists of the work necessary—such as editing, recording, and graphic production—to get a recorded television or radio show into final broadcast form. Here is a list of the major careers in these areas:

Careers, Continued

A variety of workers help create the proper setting of a television show, newscast, or movie; other workers help actors and actresses create a physical appearance that is appropriate for a broadcast. Many television stations employ *graphic artists* or *scenic designers,* who plan set designs, construct scenery, paint backdrops, and handle lettering and artwork. *Props workers* create the physical aspects of a scene for television and motion picture productions. Some larger stations have makeup artists and costumers who work with the art staff. *Costume designers* help create the look of a television show, be it a Western set in the 1800s or a modern-day medical drama set in an inner-city hospital. They research clothing styles and design or plan each actor's and actress's wardrobe. *Makeup artists* and *hairstylists* make sure that actors and actresses look the right way for a scene or broadcast.

At radio stations, *music librarians* are occasionally employed because of the heavy reliance on recorded music. This individual evaluates and often selects the music to be used for a particular show, and catalogs and stores the musical recordings.

Writers fall into different categories in broadcasting, depending on their area of work. *Screenwriters* work on actual programs, developing the words and ideas for each show. In the news division, *newswriters* may be responsible for writing the entire news section of a broadcast, or, in longer programs, they may write the introduction to news segments developed by *reporters and correspondents* (those who collect the local news and transmit live coverage). Most local television news stations have writers who write the newscasters' scripts and correspondents who write their own pieces. *Continuity writers* script commercial announcements, public service announcements, and station promotional announcements.

Animators and cartoonists create animated images in movies and on television shows such as "The Simpsons."

Television producers work behind the scenes of television programs and newscasts; they write scripts, hire staff, and bring together the many different elements of production to create a successful show. *Casting agents* are responsible for auditioning actors and actresses for television shows (and also motion pictures). Sometimes they hold open auditions; other times they may contact people they feel might be particularly good for a role.

Radio producers help to determine a radio station's identity. They research the marketplace and create radio shows to interest and entertain the targeted audience. While a disc jockey is on the air, producers keep the radio show running behind-the-scenes by keeping track of commercials, screening callers, and arranging the appearances of on-air guests such as celebrities and sports figures.

Television directors control the decisions that shape a television program, from live production and local newscasts to dramatic TV movies and sitcoms. *Directors of photography* make sure that each shoot goes as planned. They check anything that might affect the quality of a shot, such as weather conditions or lighting. *Program assistants* coordinate the various parts of a show by assisting the producer or director. They arrange for props and makeup service, prepare cue cards and scripts, and usually time rehearsals and shows. Floor staff work on the studio floor arranging sets, backdrops, and lighting, and handle the various moveable props used on the show.

Lighting directors make sure that lighting is appropriate for the mood of a television show or broadcast. *Electrical technicians,* sometimes known as *gaffers,* assist the lighting director. The *grip,* sometimes known as the *best boy,* assists the gaffer with setting up the appropriate lighting and cameras for each production.

The *floor manager* directs the performers on the studio floor in accordance with the producer/director's instructions by relaying stage directions and cues. Using a headset, he or she is in touch with the director in the control room at all times.

In the technical nerve center of a station, surrounded by racks of electronic equipment, the *broadcast engineer* brings together the various elements of the show, switching from the camera in the studio to a slide projector, then to a videotape player or a live remote, and finally to the network program usually originating in New York or Los Angeles. Broadcast engineers are supervised by the program director. Broadcast engineers also work at radio stations.

On the studio floor, engineers handle the camera and microphones as the show progresses. At the transmitter, often miles away, the *transmitter engineers,* who have final technical control over the program, monitor and adjust the complex electronic gear to ensure the strength, clarity, and reliability of the signal sent from the transmitter. All of the technical work is supervised by the *chief engineer,* a fully qualified engineer with considerable experience as a working technician. In radio, this person may be the only engineer; in television, he or she may supervise as many as forty people. The work of the chief engineer is to plan and coordinate the engineering requirements of shows, including the scheduling and assignment of crews. The chief engineer is responsible for the operation and maintenance of the equipment, makes deci-

CAREERS, CONTINUED

sions about purchasing new equipment, and often designs and develops special equipment for the station's needs.

In television production, the *video director* supervises the *video editors* who time, cut, splice, and clean tape. This person also supervises the advance screening of the videotape to determine its suitability for broadcast and participates in the decisions involving the purchase of taped shows.

Promotions, Sales, Marketing, and Community Affairs. Promotion departments publicize the station's programs, image, and activities. Headed by a *promotion manager,* such a department typically plans and directs advertising campaigns, arranges for public appearances of on-air personalities, and designs other promotional activities aimed at the station audience. The promotion department may also develop sales promotions that include the planning and layout of advertising for trade journals and production of sales brochures and other material used by sales department personnel.

Commercial radio and television stations are supported by the money received for commercial announcements and programs. *Salespeople* secure these advertising revenues. Local sales are the responsibility of the *sales manager,* who sets the general sales policy for the station and supervises the daily activities of the sales force. The sales manager develops sales plans that will appeal to sponsors, and also plans special campaigns to tie in with seasons of the year, special events, and so on.

Marketing workers help radio and television stations advertise themselves to the viewing or listening public. People working in marketing might develop a catchy phrase, like NBC's "Must-See TV," an instantly recognizable song, an eye-catching logo, or anything else that will help identify the station and attract viewers or listeners.

Local stations closely identify with their communities. *Community affairs directors* plan and execute a station's services and programs that are meant to respond to the needs of the community. These include public service announcements, public affairs programming (often undertaken in conjunction with the news department), and special events and public service campaigns that deal with community-related issues.

On-Air Careers

On-air performers, such as announcers, newscasters, sportscasters, reporters, weatherpeople, disc jockeys, and actors and actresses are the workers that the public knows best. Their work, and their personalities, help a station build a listening- or viewing-audience. Here are some of the most recognizable on-air careers:

Radio and *television anchorpeople*, sometimes known as *anchors*, analyze and broadcast news received from a variety of sources. They help select, write, and present the news.

Television and *radio reporters* and *correspondents* gather, write, and report on news events for broadcast audiences. They may conduct on-air interviews, help edit recorded footage, and report live from remote sites. They may occasionally work as anchors.

Television and *radio commentators* offer their personal opinions about current events, politics, sports, and entertainment on radio and television newscasts. *Food critics* present reviews of restaurants and food-related events for television and radio stations.

Weather forecasters compile and analyze meteorological information in order to prepare weather reports for daily and nightly newscasts. They help create graphics, write scripts, and explain weather maps to audiences. They also provide special reports during weather emergencies.

Sportscasters cover and report on sporting events for radio and television newscasts; they write, produce, and edit feature segments for broadcast.

Talk show hosts oversee daily or weekly news, comedy, or variety shows on television and radio. Game show hosts supervise contestants who compete for prizes such as cash, trips, and merchandise. *Comedians* are entertainers who make people laugh. They appear as members of ensemble casts on television shows like "Saturday Night Live," on sitcoms, talk shows, and on radio shows.

Actors and *actresses* play parts or roles in dramatic productions on television, radio, the stage, and in motion pictures. *Stuntpeople* fill in for actors and actresses when a dangerous stunt is required, such as a chase atop a moving train, a fall from a building, or a barroom brawl.

Disc jockeys introduce songs and news reports, field phone calls, and discuss current events or other topics on radio stations.

Books

Edward R. Murrow: An American Original, by Joseph E. Persico

Radio in the Television Age, by Peter Fornatale

Sportscasting, by John R. Hitchcock

Movies

Broadcast News

Good Morning Vietnam

Tootsie

Professionals Read

Billboard

Broadcasting & Cable

The Hollywood Reporter

Radio & Records

Variety

Employment Opportunities

The best place for a beginner to look for a job in radio and television is in one of the many smaller stations throughout the country. Between 1990 and 2006, some growth is expected in radio and television as new stations are licensed and the number of cable systems continues to rise. Competition will be stiff; however, jobs should be easier to find in radio because more radio stations hire beginners. Internships are an excellent way to gain experience; work at a high school or college station is also valuable.

Large stations normally require a considerable amount of broadcasting experience for nearly all jobs in the programming, engineering, and sales areas. Employees of large-market stations generally belong to unions, and thus earn higher salaries than their nonunion counterparts.

Smaller stations, particularly those in smaller communities, are often willing to hire individuals with less experience. Many people establish roots in smaller communities and develop highly satisfactory careers. Others, after they have acquired an understanding of radio and television operations and skill at their particular job, move on to larger stations in larger communities where the financial rewards are greater. It is possible to get a beginning job at a network, but networks have many more applicants than openings. Although they may occasionally hire inexperienced people, it happens very rarely.

Much of the production work for TV and radio programs is taken on by freelance workers; directors, producers, writers, and others hire on with networks, stations, or independent production companies to cover sporting and entertainment events, radio programs, or to create documentaries and news specials.

Fast Facts

During a microphone test before a 1984 radio broadcast, President Ronald Reagan said, "My fellow Americans, I am pleased to tell you I just signed legislation which outlaws Russia forever. The bombing begins in five minutes." He didn't realize he was actually on the air.

Industry Outlook

Are you ready for DentistryTV? Or the All Jell-O Channel? This may be in the future of television, as advancements in technology allow for more cable channels than ever—between two hundred and five hundred. Even a network TV program as popular as "ER" doesn't draw as many viewers as a top-rated network program of ten years ago; this is the result of competition for the TV viewer, a competition that will continue to determine the state of the broadcast industry. As more cable channels develop, so will more network television affiliates, all vying for the fickle attention of the viewing public. This, obviously, will provide more work for people in broadcasting. "Narrowcasting" is also likely to increase, offering job opportunities for people in radio and TV. Narrowcasting involves producing programming for a specific community, such as educational programs for schools, or health programs for hospitals and doctors' offices.

> **"The one function TV news performs very well is that when there is no news, we give it to you with the same emphasis as if there were."**
> **—David Brinkley**

The broadcast industry is also expecting heavier competition from the home personal computer; Internet subscribers are spending a combined total of 12.8 million hours per week on-line visiting over eighty thousand Web sites, and this number is increasing every day. Many in the industry aren't that concerned about a loss of viewers—they see the Internet as way to better reach their viewers. Eventually, TV may become more interactive, allowing viewers to schedule their own programming, purchase products directly from advertisers, and receive up-to-the-minute news and information. Currently, thousands of local radio stations have Web pages; this may eventually translate into radio stations transmitting their programs internationally via the Internet.

Though the number of women and minorities working in the broadcast industry has increased, and will likely continue to increase, analysts are not expecting big changes in the next century. Women and minorities still face discrimination and prejudice in the workplace—many women earn lower salaries than men in the same careers. Ideally, the percentage of minorities working in the industry would reflect the percentage of minorities in the general population; unless the industry radically changes its hiring practices, this balance won't be struck anytime within the next fifty years. Some organizations are attempting to bring more minorities into the industry: The National Association of Broadcasters offers financial assistance to minorities looking to buy into broadcast properties, and also offers job placement services. The Broadcasting Training Program is also an organization assisting minorities by offering valuable training opportunities.

Section 2

WHAT DO I NEED TO KNOW ABOUT

Careers?

radio & TV

Broadcast Engineer

SUMMARY

DEFINITION
Broadcast engineers *operate and maintain the electronic equipment used to record and transmit the audio signals for radio and the audio and visual signals for television. They may work in a broadcasting station or assist in broadcasting directly from an outside site.*

ALTERNATIVE JOB TITLES
Broadcast operator
Broadcast technician
Field technician
Maintenance technician
Video control technician
Video-robo technician
Video technician

SALARY RANGE
$18,000 to $35,000 to $60,000

EDUCATIONAL REQUIREMENTS
High school diploma; two years of training at junior college or a technical school

CERTIFICATION OR LICENSING
Voluntary

EMPLOYMENT OUTLOOK
About as fast as the average

HIGH SCHOOL SUBJECTS
Computer science
Mathematics
Shop (Trade/Vo-tech education)

PERSONAL INTERESTS
Broadcasting
Building things
Figuring out how things work
Fixing things
Travel

"Five . . . four . . . three . . ." The director counts down to show time, the anchors seated on the set and poised to begin the show. ". . . two, and one . . . roll and up . . ." The darkened screen comes alive with the graphics and music of the local news program broadcast live across the city. ". . . camera two—focus it . . ." With that direction the video-robo engineer moves camera two into position and brings its image, a close-up, into sharp focus. ". . . take two . . . " The technical director switches to the second camera, from the close-up to a shot of both anchors. To achieve a smooth cut the anchor looks into the second camera at exactly the right moment. ". . . and roll." The video recording engineer begins a prerecorded videotape that has been precisely timed to run as long as the anchor's copy.

WHAT DOES A BROADCAST ENGINEER DO?

Broadcast engineers, sometimes known as *broadcast technicians,* set up and operate the equipment used to record and transmit television programs. They install the equipment, keep it in working order, and repair the equipment when necessary. Broadcast engineers work in particular departments, such as news

What Does a Broadcast Engineer Do?, continued

or sports, or for an individual program. Depending on their assignments, engineers work in studios and other controlled environments, or they may go out into the field. For anyone interested in a career in broadcast engineering, there are several different specialties to choose from.

With the introduction of robotic cameras, stations no longer need to employ an engineer for every camera. Instead, a *video-robo technician* will direct the camera's movements via computer. Video-robo technicians are also responsible for the "look" of the broadcast image. Using a video panel with joysticks assigned to each camera, the engineer pans and tilts the camera, and fine-tunes its focus.

Often it is necessary to broadcast live from a "remote"—a site outside the studio. Reporters may also need to record material at a remote site for later broadcast. Shooting outside the studio is the responsibility of the *field technicians*. Once at the remote site, the technicians transmit to the station through telephone wires. After the transmission is connected, they connect any microphones or amplifiers that may be needed. If the engineers cannot use telephone wires, they will set up and operate microwave transmitters to broadcast to the station.

Lingo to Learn

Character generating: The positioning of typed text on a broadcast image.

Page: An individual preprogrammed computer screen assigned to a camera and used to control the camera's movements.

Panning: Rotating a camera horizontally.

Remote: A broadcast being taped outside a station's studio.

Rundown: A second-by-second breakdown of a program's schedule.

Tilting: Moving a camera vertically.

No matter how advanced the equipment becomes, there will always be a need for competent maintenance support. *Maintenance technicians* are responsible for ensuring that every camera, microphone, transmitter, amplifier, and any cables used by the station are in working order. Assisting the maintenance technicians are the *technical stock clerks* who order all the necessary equipment.

Video technicians continue to work in the control rooms of stations that are nonautomated, and they are responsible for adjusting the visual quality of the picture. Using a control panel for each camera and monitors in the control room, a video technician adjusts the focus and sharpness of the picture before it is broadcast.

During a live broadcast, such as a news program, videotapes recorded at an earlier time may be aired. Usually, these tapes have been recorded by technicians; however, with the increasing accessibility of video camcorders, tapes recorded by the public are often used. *Video recording technicians* work with the producer to insure that the recorded tapes play at the appointed time during the live broadcast. For example, while a news anchor reads the copy, the video recording technician will play the recorded material accompanying that story. These technicians will often create their own sound and special effects.

Working in the master control room, the transmitter operator monitors and logs the transmitter signals sending out the actual broadcast. Every broadcasting station is assigned a specific frequency, and it is the responsibility of the transmitter operator to supervise the station's transmission. The *chief engineer* is responsible for the station's entire technical operations, including the station's technical budget. A successful chief engineer will often have several years of experience, as well as an advanced education. Working with a *scheduling assistant*, the chief engineer assigns projects to the technicians and is responsible for making sure that the station is running smoothly. The chief engineer is also responsible for hiring new employees and supervising the work of the entry-level technicians.

What Is It Like to Be a Broadcast Engineer?

Breaking stories, last-minute edits, screaming producers: these are the highly stressful elements of producing broadcast news; for Tony Palos, a video-robo engineer at WMAQ, the NBC affiliate in Chicago, Illinois, these elements have become part of a daily routine.

At the beginning of his shift at 3:00 PM, Tony checks the working order of the robotic cameras. He also works with the lighting crew to determine the best position for the cameras, taking into consideration the different anchor personnel who will be reporting that day's news.

Once the cameras are set, the technicians begin to record videotapes needed for the 4:30 PM news program. The videotape and accompanying copy are timed by the producer and video recording technician to ensure that the newscast has the correct running time. After the script has been written, the director will decide what type of shot will be used with each news story and then formulate a rundown for that day's show.

The director is in charge of calling the shots, while the technical director puts the commands into action, actually pushing the buttons that change the broadcast picture. From the several monitors in the control room during the program, the directors choose the specific shots to be used. The director's orders are carried to the various engineering rooms by a speaker system.

What Is It Like to Be a . . . ?, continued

As the video-robo engineer, Tony sits in a separate control room from the technical director and director. With the different monitors in his office, he checks the studio floor, the camera shots, and the picture being broadcast live. He controls the three robotic cameras with a computerized touch screen. The camera's movements are manipulated by preprogrammed screens, called pages, that are assigned to each camera.

Standing approximately six feet tall, with automated legs, the robotic cameras resemble characters from science fiction movies. Each stands on black-and-white tiles called "home base," and all movements are determined relative to that spot on the floor. For example, during a news broadcast one camera will have to move away from the anchor table to the area where the weather forecasts are taped. To move the camera, Tony hits the button on that camera's computerized page to move it in the required pattern. By manipulating joysticks on the video panel, Tony moves the camera in a pan or tilt action. He is also responsible for the quality of the broadcast image and uses the panel to adjust the focus, shadow, and scope of the image.

With the introduction of the robotic technology, the engineering staff has been reduced from 180 to 100 people. Before its introduction, a camera operator and a video engineer were needed for each camera. Because of the sophistication of the technology and proficiency of the video-robo engineers, quality has not suffered.

Tony has worked with NBC in various positions for seventeen years. Prior to working in the control room as a video-robo engineer, he worked for NBC Sports as a field technician, a job he describes as a "blast."

Indeed, for someone who enjoys traveling a great deal, working as a field technician can be very exciting; for Tony that excitement took the form of covering Super Bowls and other major sporting events. The engineering crew often stays at the same hotels as the athletes and can share in the festivities.

On the other hand, field work can be physically demanding. "A lot of the glamour that people think is there, really isn't," Tony says. To cover a football game that starts at noon, the engineering crew's day begins at 5:30 in the morning. In stadiums designed without cable modification, technicians run all the wires as well as construct and mount the camera equipment. Because a camera operator may be assigned to cover a particular player on both the offense and defense (for replay and close-up purposes), he or she may spend the whole day taping a game and never see a minute of live action. The day doesn't end until all of the camera equipment has been taken down; by then the stadium is almost empty. "It would be us and the cleaning crew," Tony says.

Have I Got What It Takes to Be a Broadcast Engineer?

It takes a team effort to successfully broadcast televised news. Each team member needs to be a professional with years of experience. "You can't do it twice," Tony says. "The news is live."

> ❝ **You can't do it twice. The news is live.**

Manual dexterity and excellent vision and color perception are important to broadcast engineers; successful broadcast engineers must also be extremely dedicated to their careers. As they struggle to air the latest-breaking news before the competition, producers and directors can become short-tempered and quick to criticize. Experienced engineers don't let the yelling get to them. In fact, a smart engineer will view these experiences as opportunities to learn, in order to avoid the wrath of the producer and director in the future.

Also, television stations are like hospitals: they never close. Someone must always be there as long as the station is broadcasting programs. Even though Tony has worked with NBC for many years, he is still occasionally scheduled to work holidays. "You can have forty years here and you'll be working Christmas Day," he says.

Tony takes great pride in his work, and has a lot of respect for his co-workers. He knows they are dedicated professionals who share his commitment to produce the best work possible. "Working with the best people from New York and California" is one of the things Tony enjoys most about his job. "These people love their work."

To be a successful broadcast engineer, you should:

- Pay strong attention to detail
- Be a team player, who can also work independently
- Be able to handle the stress of working in all kinds of environments
- Enjoy working with highly technical electronic and computer equipment

How Do I Become a Broadcast Engineer?

Tony was already working for NBC when he was in high school. He focused on auto mechanics, but as he gained experience at NBC, he became more and more interested in broadcast technology.

Who Will Hire Me?

The most important and difficult step for the entry-level engineer is getting a foot in the door. Tony began working for NBC as a part-time assistant in the guest relations department, where he answered telephones and took viewer comments. From guest relations he moved up to a technical porter's position, helping to clean up the minicam shop. He gained important experience the following year when he started working as a technical stock clerk.

Eventually, Tony was allowed to work part-time as a cameraman. For four years he went back and forth between the stock room and the studio. When he finally decided he wanted a career in engineering, he applied to the DeVry Institute of Technology. The station helped him with the tuition.

For most entry-level engineers, their careers begin in the smaller markets. Beginning engineers may deal heavily with maintenance, but because smaller stations are often nonunion, their responsibilities could cover several different areas.

Advancement Possibilities

Chief engineers direct and coordinate radio or television station activities concerned with acquisition, installation, and maintenance, or with modification of studio broadcasting equipment.

Producers plan and coordinate various aspects of radio, television, or cable television programs.

Technical directors coordinate activities of radio or television studio and control-room personnel to ensure technical quality of picture and sound for programs originating in studio or from remote pickup points.

Working in smaller markets is considered an excellent opportunity for entry-level engineers to discover their own strengths and weaknesses and to help them decide in which field of broadcasting to specialize. There is less intense pressure on the technical crew in smaller markets, and the beginning engineer can learn how programs are produced, including the proper use of lighting, the most effective use of camera angles, and the interrelationship of the various departments in a television station. Once an engineer understands the production process, he or she can anticipate the demands that the producer may have in the future.

The chief engineer of the station will carefully supervise the work of the new engineers. However, once their competence has been proven, new engineers work independently or even supervise the newer engineers.

When broadcast engineers want to advance in their careers, they send out tapes of programs they've worked on, tapes that demonstrate their skills with lighting, shooting, or editing. The field is very competitive, and it takes persistence on the part of the broadcast engineer to break into the larger markets. Success depends on the engineer's qualifications, dedication, and enthusiasm. "If they really have their heart set on it they will probably do all right,"

Tony says about ambitious people pursuing work as broadcast engineers. "Someone who really has the desire will find a place."

The Society of Broadcast Engineers, Inc., offers its members a job line that lists broadcast engineering jobs in all parts of the country. Also, the National Association of Broadcasters, in Washington, DC, offers a job line through its Employment Clearinghouse (see "Look to the Pros" at the end of this book).

WHERE CAN I GO FROM HERE?

Experienced engineers can move on to positions as supervisory technicians or chief engineers. A college degree in engineering is generally required to become a chief engineer at a large TV station. Other possibilities for advancement include becoming a technical director or a producer.

WHAT ARE SOME RELATED JOBS?

Related Jobs

Camera operators
Communications coordinators
Film developers
Radio/telephone operators
Radiographers
Videographers

The U.S. Department of Labor classifies broadcast engineers under the headings, Radio Operators and Sound, Film, and Videotape Recording, and Reproduction Occupations (DOT) and Engineering Technology: Electrical/Electronic and Crafts: Reproduction (GOE). Also under these headings are people who work with engraving machines, photofinishing equipment printing presses, and other equipment used to reproduce images, as well as people who work with communications equipment in the radio and television industry. Other related jobs include communications coordinators, camera operators, radio/telephone operators, film developers, radiographers, and videographers.

WHAT ARE THE SALARY RANGES?

Salaries vary a great deal among the various technical jobs; salaries are also determined by the size of the market. Engineers in radio generally make less than those in TV. Beginning broadcast engineers can expect to earn between $17,000 to $19,000 per year. Because entry-level engineers working at smaller

What Are the Salary Ranges?, continued

stations accrue a great deal of overtime, however, their yearly salaries could be as high as $32,000.

As engineers move to the larger markets their salaries can be higher by almost two-thirds. Engineers receive the highest wages in the cities of New York, Los Angeles, Chicago, and Washington, DC. Salary ranges also break down along lines of responsibilities, with maintenance engineers earning between $25,000 to $50,000. Engineers in supervisory roles have extra responsibilities and therefore earn higher salaries. Technical directors and chief engineers in the larger markets can earn up to $60,000.

What Is the Job Outlook?

The job outlook for broadcasting engineers is expected to grow about as fast as the average for all occupations into the next century. The number of new radio and television stations will continue to grow, and qualified engineers will be in demand, specially in smaller towns and cities. This demand will be tempered somewhat by the development of new equipment technology. As Tony's experience at NBC demonstrates, demand for engineers to perform conventional duties will diminish as stations become more computerized.

Some engineers may find work outside of broadcasting. As the new technology becomes more accessible, new industries are discovering the usefulness of visual communications. More and more corporations are creating in-house communications departments to produce their own corporate and industrial videos. Videos effectively explain company policies ranging from public safety (aimed at their customers) to first aid (aimed at their employees). Also, videos of high quality can introduce a company to potential clients in the best light.

Fast Fact

Television monitors are often placed on the camera sideline carts at football games for the fans whose views are blocked by the camera.

In addition to industrial work, videographers are in great demand today for the production of commercials, animation, and computer graphics. The field of videography is changing rapidly with the introduction of new and cheaper computer systems and desktop software packages: with advanced multimedia computer systems the user can edit and lay down sound tracks via a computer. Maintenance workers will always be in demand, even with the new technology. Someone will always have to be on hand to fix broken equipment and to keep new equipment in good working order.

Radio Producers and Disc Jockeys

SUMMARY

DEFINITION
The work of radio producers and disc jockeys determine a radio station's identity. Producers and disc jockeys research the marketplace and create radio shows to interest and entertain the targeted audience. While on the air, disc jockeys introduce songs and news reports, field phone calls, and discuss current events.

ALTERNATIVE JOB TITLES
*Announcer
DJ
On-air personality
Program director*

SALARY RANGE
$16,000 to $30,000 to $200,000+

EDUCATIONAL REQUIREMENTS
Some postsecondary training

CERTIFICATION OR LICENSING
None

EMPLOYMENT OUTLOOK
Faster than the average

HIGH SCHOOL SUBJECTS
*Journalism
Music
Speech*

PERSONAL INTERESTS
*Business
Current events
Entertaining/Performing
Theater*

A cup of coffee in hand, Ken Holiday leans forward to discuss the morning's newspaper headlines with the other men in the room. But this isn't the corner coffee shop, where the words of their conversation will get lost in the noise of scraping forks and the chatter of other diners—what these men have to say will reach a wide Florida audience. Sitting with Ken are Surfboy, Stuntboy, and Ballpark Frank, the sportscaster, each with his own microphone.

Ken stifles a yawn, relying on Surfboy and Stuntboy to carry on the discussion for a second or two. It's only a little after 6:00 AM, and already he's been up preparing for the show for two hours. But he knows he has to be cheerful, as well as careful about what he says. His thoughts, and those of the other radio personalities in the booth, will be broadcast into the cars, kitchens, and bedrooms of men and women all across the city starting their day.

What Do Radio Producers and Disc Jockeys Do?

If you listen to your car radio when you drive, you've noticed how the conversations and opinions of radio disc jockeys dominate the airwaves. And you probably have a favorite station and morning show. Some disc jockeys may drive you crazy, while others entertain you and help you keep your sense of humor as you get ready for school or bide your time in a traffic jam—they even provide you with live traffic reports so you can avoid those jams. Where do you have your car radio or home stereo dial set, and why? Do you prefer a serious news report in the morning? A live interview? Jokes and discussions about current events? A sunny personality, or a dark one? Maybe you just want somebody to tell you the names of the songs they're playing, and nothing else. The identity and style of a radio program is a result of the collaborations of on-air and off-air professionals. Radio disc jockeys talk the talk during a broadcast, and producers walk the walk behind the scenes. But in many situations, particularly with smaller radio stations, the disc jockey and the show's producer are the same person.

Radio producers rely on the public's very particular tastes—differences in taste allow for many different kinds of radio to exist, to serve many different segments of a community. In developing radio programs, producers take into consideration the marketplace—they listen to other area radio stations and determine what's needed and appreciated in the community, and what there may already be too much of. They conduct surveys and interviews to find out what the public wants to hear. They decide which age groups they want to pursue, and develop a format based on what appeals to these listeners. This all results in a station's "identity," which is very important. Listeners associate a station with the kind of music it plays, how much music it plays, and the station's on-air personalities.

Disc jockeys are generally well known within their community, and they frequently interact with their listeners. In addition to making many public appearances for promotional and charity events, radio disc jockeys are often approached by their listeners on the street. These listeners express their opinions about what they want to hear in the program. Based on this feedback, and

Lingo to Learn

Aircheck: Tape recordings of radio broadcasts; used by disc jockeys and producers as samples of their work.

Demographics: Statistics that show a radio listener's age, income, and other data; this information is valuable to producers and advertisers trying to reach specific audiences.

Digital broadcasting: Broadcasting radio programs with the digital technology used in computers and compact discs. Provides higher quality broadcasts.

Mixing: Blending sounds by editing and splicing; usually done with computer.

Playlist: A list of songs to be played throughout the day by a radio station; composed by a disc jockey, programmer, or producer.

DJs in radio history

Sybil Herrold One of the first women announcers in radio, Herrold taught courses in Morse Code at a college in San Jose, California. Her interest in radio transmission was shared by her husband, Charles, who owned a radio station. In 1912, about 10 years before radio announcing became commonplace, Herrold played records and announced at her husband's station.

Arthur Godfrey Godfrey is famous for a long career as a TV variety show host; before that, he made a name for himself in radio as one of the first announcers to assert his personality. Up until the late 1920s, announcers spoke on the air only occasionally. Godfrey, however, frequently expressed his opinions on-air about the station's music and commercials.

Alan Freed While announcing for a rhythm-and-blues radio station in Cleveland, Freed introduced the phrase "rock and roll." But that's not the only newly coined phrase to mark his career—in 1959, he was accused of taking "payola," or payment for playing records.

Wolfman Jack Even before he got involved in radio, Jack was dedicated to bringing rock, and rhythm and blues to the people, even embarking on the risky venture of an integrated dance club in the racially tense South of the early 1960s. Jack worked under many different names at many different stations before gaining fame at XERB-AM in Mexico, attracting fans in Southern California. Songs were written for him, and he was featured in the film "American Graffiti."

on market research, radio disc jockeys/producers devise music playlists and music libraries. They each develop an individual on-air identity, or personality. And they invite guests who will interest their listeners. Keeping a show running on time is also the responsibility of a producer. This involves carefully weaving many different elements into a show, including music, news reports, traffic reports, and interviews.

In addition to keeping in touch with the listening public, radio disc jockeys and producers also keep track of current events. They consult newspapers and other radio programs to determine what subjects to discuss on their morning shows. They also take phone calls from listeners, discussions which are often broadcast live during a show.

Promotions are important to the staff of a radio station. The on-air personalities are often involved in community events to promote the stations. Radio producers write copy for on-air commercials. They also devise contests, from large public events to small, on-air trivia competitions.

Though a majority of radio stations have music formats, radio producers also work for twenty-four-hour news stations, public broadcasting, and talk radio. Producing news programs and radio documentaries involves a great deal of research, booking guests, writing scripts, and interviewing.

What Is It Like to Be a Radio Producer or Disc Jockey?

Ken Holiday works as morning show announcer and program director for WBVD, a classic rock station in Melbourne, Florida. During the morning show's live broadcast, Ken is surrounded by "three goofy-looking guys, too ugly for TV,"

What Is It Like to Be a . . . ?, continued

he says. The four of them, with nothing else in the room but a computer, four microphones, and a vintage reel-to-reel tape player, entertain commuters and other radio listeners as early as 6:00 AM.

"I start my day at 4:00 AM," he says, "so that I can sound happy at 6:00 AM." He must also prepare himself for the program by reading the newspaper to get an idea of the day's topics of conversation. He also does a fair amount of producing in those early hours, getting together with the other staff members to plan the show. "But 90 percent doesn't get on the air," he says, because of the number of live phone calls and on-air discussion.

Ken isn't actually "spinning the records" during the live broadcast; there are no CDs or any other recorded music in the studio. Ken has already programmed the music for the full day, leaving some open slots for requests. Scheduling the station's playlist involves paying close attention to the listening audience. Judging from phone-in requests, a suggestion line, and by keeping in touch with listeners through public events outside the station, Ken is able to determine what music his audience wants to hear. "I try to get into the listener's mind," he says. Ken also hears about his listeners' dislikes; every day he spends four and a half hours in his office, and part of that time is spent answering complaints. "The jocks may have hurt somebody's feelings," he says. It is Ken's responsibility to keep his listeners interested in the morning show and the station, to keep them happy with the playlist and the on-air personalities.

Long hours are typical for Ken—he generally works twelve-hour days, five days a week, in addition to doing at least one live broadcast every weekend. He's also involved in charity work, using his on-air influence to bring recognition to such groups as the New Hope Children's Wish Foundation, for which he cut an album of fourteen songs. He sold one thousand copies of his album and donated the proceeds to the organization.

Tracy Straitz is also involved in classic rock radio in Florida, but she has been working freelance for ten years. In addition to multimedia consulting work, she is a radio producer and on-air personality. Tracy is currently developing a new radio show based on research she compiled producing a previous show. "I studied the demographics and the music tastes within the market and have discovered some huge gaping holes," she says. "Many of them are due to radio station buyouts which are occurring as quickly in this marketplace as anyone can ever remember." These buyouts, she explains, heavily affect programming, staffing, and production. "This is a nightmare for the advertisers and listeners because the end product can be developed by out-of-towners who might have a keen understanding of making money, and of radio, but they often come in without knowing anything about the marketplace they have just bought a station in."

Aware of how damaging ignorance of a community can be to a radio program and advertising, Tracy has a clear plan of how to develop a successful radio show. "You have to develop a very specific focus and concept for your show," she says. "Then you have to determine if there is a place to house it: which station and format. You have to study the market and see if the demographics match your concept well enough to sell through to the advertisers." This involves Tracy developing a hypothetical scenario including a start-date for a show, along with a summary of all the other details. "It reads like a mini-business plan," she says. "Then you shop it to potential advertisers and encourage them to give you nonbinding commitments of 'intent to advertise' on the show." With these commitments in hand, a producer can go to a chosen station. "Usually nobody in their right mind turns down money."

Tracy is currently in the research stage of developing her program, which can take six to nine months. But she has an idea of what she wants the show to be. "I noticed a very disturbing trend in the Miami marketplace a year ago," she says. "Many of the stations that had offered classic rock for eons jumped ship to alternative format." Tracy saw this as a disastrous move for the marketplace; through her research, she has determined that members of "Generation X" to whom alternative music generally appeals, are not as reliable and dedicated music listeners as baby-boomers. "My show will be an updated version of the last show I had—an all-vinyl rock show. People will have the opportunity to help program the show on-line. They will have the chance to come in as guest DJs, and I will do on-location shows once a month." If everything works out, Tracy hopes to broadcast the show live on the radio and the Internet at the same time. "If it's successful here, I plan to syndicate."

HAVE I GOT WHAT IT TAKES TO BE A PRODUCER OR DJ?

Working as the on-air personality for a live show requires you to think fast and speak clearly. You should also have a love for radio and a commitment to radio listeners. Whether producing behind the scenes or juggling all the elements of a broadcast while live on the air, you need to have organizational skills. You must be able to remain calm in the face of stressful situations.

Ken gives credit for his on-air success to his partners. "When you start to see someone sink," he says, "you help them out." Things can get stressful, such as when getting a good promotion off the ground. "And there's a ratings

Have I Got What It Takes?, continued

book that judges you every day," he says. But these stresses are made up for by the added benefits of working in radio. "I've taken special trips to Cleveland for the Rock and Roll Hall of Fame broadcast," he says, and he also has the opportunity to interview performers such as Mick Jagger and Gregg Allman backstage at concerts.

Tracy also appreciates those added benefits. "You get to attend a lot of things for free as a radio personality," she says. "If you work as an on-location radio personality, you're having a blast and making money too." But Tracy is concerned about the way radio stations try to make do with too few departments and employees. "Down here, the account executives/salespeople usually have to sell the advertising, write the commercial, and most probably, record the commercial. In a properly run station, these are all separate departments." Though Tracy has not had trouble with wearing many different hats in a production, some people have difficulty managing more than one area of business.

To be a successful radio producer or disc jockey, you should:

Have a strong, clear speaking voice (disc jockey)
Be eager to learn
Be able to think quickly and remain calm during stressful situations
Love communicating and interacting with others
Be organized
Have a good understanding of all aspects of a radio station, from management to advertising to promotions to news and traffic departments
Be yourself on the air

How Do I Become a Radio Producer or Disc Jockey?

Training has never actually stopped for Ken. "You can never stop learning in this business," he says. Though he started broadcasting school, he didn't finish; instead, he went right to work for a radio station. "You've got to be well-rounded and topical. Your personality evolves over time. A lot of jocks try to be someone they've listened to, like Howard Stern. But you've got to be yourself."

Tracy says, "Understanding how radio works is a real trick. I have a much better understanding now because the first station I was on staff with sent me to additional training." This training was with the Radio Association of Broadcasters, an organization with a great deal of resource material in marketing.

Education

High School

Writing skills are valuable in any profession, but especially in radio and television. Take composition and literature courses, and other courses that require essays and term papers. Journalism courses will not only help you develop your writing skills, but will teach you about the nature and history of media. You'll learn about deadlines, and how to put a complete project (such as a newspaper or yearbook) together. If your school has a radio station, get involved with it in any way you can. Check with your local radio stations; some may offer part-time jobs to high school students interested in becoming producers and disc jockeys.

> "A lot of jocks try to be someone they've listened to, like Howard Stern. But you've got to be yourself."

Business courses and clubs frequently require students to put together projects; starting any business is similar to producing your own radio show. Use such a project as an opportunity to become familiar with the market research, interviewing, and writing that are all part of a radio producer's job. For both the future radio producer and the future disc jockey, a theater department offers great learning opportunities. Theater productions require funding, advertising, and other fundamentals similar to a radio production. In training for a career as a disc jockey, you can develop improvisational and speaking skills.

Postsecondary Training
Most journalism and communications schools at universities offer programs in broadcasting. Radio producers and announcers often start their training in journalism schools, and receive hands-on instruction at campus radio stations. These broadcasting programs are generally news-centered, providing great opportunities for students interested in producing news programs, daily newscasts, and documentaries. News directors and program managers of radio stations generally want to hire people who have a good, well-rounded education with a grounding of history, geography, political science, and literature.

Someone interested in becoming a disc jockey may benefit as much from a part-time radio job as from a college program. Being directly involved in the workplace provides you with valuable experience, and chances to produce tapes of your work. On-air personalities are often hired on the basis of their personalities, and enthusiasm, perseverance, and good speaking skills are valuable to people looking to be part of a radio show.

INTERNSHIPS AND VOLUNTEERSHIPS

While in high school, you may have an opportunity to work as a summer intern for a local radio station. Though you may be selling advertising, fielding phone calls, or assisting the staff in various other ways, some stations may provide you with some on-air experience. AM stations that broadcast local high school sports events may use interns to give the on-air play-by-play. Any on-air experience, from reading a list of community events to giving a news report will allow staff members to hear your voice and to provide helpful instruction. In many cases, interns, and part-time employees, can get full-time jobs if they show initiative and interest.

If enrolled in a broadcasting program at a college, you may have many internship opportunities. Some colleges bring in internship recruiters from radio stations across the country. When gathering information about journalism colleges, make sure you ask for detailed information about their internship programs. If you must pursue internships on your own, call all your local radio stations and check the Internet for internship opportunities in other cities. If you have a favorite national radio program, contact them about internships; though competition for an internship with a national program will be fierce, the internship could prove very valuable to your career.

Advancement possibilities

TV news anchors *lead the broadcast on-camera; they read the news and introduce live and taped news segments.*

General sales managers *head the marketing departments of radio stations; they direct staffs of salespeople who generate station revenue.*

Station managers *lead all the departments of radio stations toward financial goals; they are actively involved in sales and promotions.*

LABOR UNIONS

In most smaller markets, on-air personalities aren't required to belong to the American Federation of Television and Radio Artists (AFTRA); the networks and the TV and radio stations in larger cities do require union membership. AFTRA, comprised of dues-paying actors, announcers, DJs, newscasters, editors, writers, directors, and vocalists, has seventy-seven thousand members across the country. The union acts as an advocate for better wages, working conditions, and benefits. It isn't necessary to join AFTRA until you have hired on with a station that requires membership.

Who Will Hire Me?

While working on a project in broadcasting school, Ken was offered a part-time job with WBVD. Within a year the job became full-time. Ken has kept this position for seventeen years, through three owners and five formats for the station. Tracy became involved in radio after working as a record producer. She went to work on the staff of two different stations to learn how they operate. "The second station is where I developed and marketed my own radio show," she says. Tracy recommends her approach to those without a broadcasting background. "There are very specific jobs available for beginners and they are the best place to start," she says. "The reality is, no matter how much schooling you have, your best experience is practical application and hands-on learning."

Radio producers and disc jockeys usually start work at radio stations in any capacity possible. After working for a while in a part-time position gaining experience and making connections, a dedicated, young producer will find opportunities to work in production or on-air. For staff positions, producers and disc jockeys submit taped samples of their on-air work to radio stations along with their resume.

Where Can I Go from Here?

Ken is happy in his current position, though people have encouraged him to move into bigger markets. "I'm paid well," he says. "I'm content. The minute I'm not content, I'll go to a bigger market."

Working freelance frees Tracy up to pursue other ambitions. She's a member of a rock band, and writes contemporary classical music. She plans on continuing with her consulting and radio producing while also taking on projects that will allow her to exercise her musical talents.

After working their way up within a station, some disc jockeys choose to move to bigger cities for the larger audiences and better pay. Or, with their experience in broadcasting, disc jockeys and producers can move into management positions.

Related Jobs

Actors
Artist-and-repertoire managers
Broadcast meteorologists
Comedians
Radio and television traffic reporters
Reporters
Public-address announcers
Public relations workers
Sportscasters
Stage managers
Television directors

What Are Some Related Jobs?

The U.S. Department of Labor classifies radio producers and disc jockeys under the heading, Occupations in Entertainment and Recreation, Not Elsewhere Classified (DOT). Other careers that fall under this classification include comedians, motion-picture directors, television directors, artist-and-repertoire (A & R) managers, casting directors, stage managers, and public-address announcers. Related careers that require strong oral communication skills include broadcast meteorologists, sportscasters, radio and television traffic reporters, reporters, public relations workers, teachers, actors, sales workers, and interpreters.

What Are the Salary Ranges?

Because the size of radio stations varies greatly, so does the pay for disc jockeys and producers. A disc jockey's popularity also determines salary—some disc jockeys are credited with attracting the bulk of a radio program's audience, good ratings, and advertising revenue. Popular disc jockeys in major markets make well over $200,000 a year. Such salaries are reserved for the very few, however; most disc jockeys average about $30,000 a year.

Both disc jockeys and producers start at around $16,000 (or less, with smaller stations), working up to $55,000 after several years' experience.

What Is the Job Outlook?

In the past, radio station ownership was highly regulated by the government, limiting the number of stations a person or company could own. Recent deregulation has made multiple station ownership possible. Radio stations now are bought and sold at a more rapid pace. This may result in a radio station changing formats, as well as entire staffs. Though some radio producers and disc jockeys are able to stay at a station over a period of several years, people going into radio should be prepared to change locations at some point in their careers.

You should also be prepared for heavier competition for radio jobs. Graduates of college broadcasting programs are finding a scarcity of work in media. Paid internships will also be difficult to find—many students of radio will have to work for free for a while to gain experience. Radio producers may find more opportunities as freelancers, developing their own programs independently then selling them to stations.

Radio and Television Anchors

SUMMARY

DEFINITION
Radio and television anchorpeople analyze and broadcast news received from various sources. They help select, write, and present the news and may specialize in a particular area.

ALTERNATIVE JOB TITLES
Announcer
Newscaster
Newsperson

SALARY RANGE
Radio: $10,000 to $26,200 to $85,000
Television: $14,000 to $54,100 to $400,000+

EDUCATIONAL REQUIREMENTS
Bachelor's degree

CERTIFICATION OR LICENSING
None

EMPLOYMENT OUTLOOK
About as fast as the average

HIGH SCHOOL SUBJECTS
Economics
English (writing/literature)
Political science
Speech

PERSONAL INTERESTS
Broadcasting
Current Events
Film and Television
Reading/Books
Writing

The crisp, modern lines of the building's silver exterior hide the beehive of activity within. The set is cool in the absence of the heat from the one thousand-watt light bulbs that are used during the newscast. Although the anchor desk is empty, just a few doors away, keyboards are clicking out scripts, film is being edited, and Lis Daily is preparing for her special noon news segment, Positively Indiana.

The desks in the newsroom are piled with papers and press releases, fifteen television sets project fifteen different images, and the assignment board is full of times, subjects, places, and deadlines. In a few hours, the chaos of the preparation will come together for a concise, professional, and relaxed newscast. Even then, the harried pace will not stop, but continue twenty-four hours a day, seven days a week, to bring the news to the people of central Indiana.

What Does a Radio or Television Anchor Do?

Radio and television anchorpeople announce the news during regular and special broadcasts. While some of the people in this field simply announce, many do a wide variety of tasks, depending on the size of the station and the market.

Anchorpeople are faced with constant deadlines, not only for each newscast to begin, but also for each one to end. Each segment must be viewed and each script must be read at the precise time and for a specified duration during the newscast. While they must appear calm, professional, and confident, there is often much stress and tension behind the scenes.

Anchorpeople open and close each news show, identify the station, and announce the station breaks. They help to write the scripts, rewrite news releases, and identify which news should be covered in the broadcast. Anchorpeople may also report the news, produce special segments, and conduct on-the-air interviews and panel discussions. At small stations, they may even keep the program log, run the transmitter, and cue the changeover to network broadcasting.

Although they perform similar jobs, radio and television anchorpeople work in very different atmospheres. On radio, the main announcers or anchorpeople are also the disc jockeys. They play recorded music, announce the news, provide informal commentary, and serve as a bridge between the music and the listener. They announce the time, weather, news, and traffic reports while maintaining a cheerful and relaxed attitude. At most stations, the radio announcers also read advertising information or provide the voices for the advertising spots.

Lingo to Learn

Market number: The size of each market as ranked by Nielsen Ratings.

Script: The written copy that is read by the anchorpeople and reporters.

TelePrompTer: A machine where the script is projected so the anchors can read it.

Some anchorpeople specialize in sports, on either radio or television. These people cover sports events and must be highly knowledgeable about the sports they are covering as well as having an ability to describe events quickly and accurately as they unfold.

Sports anchors generally travel to the events they cover and spend time watching the teams or individuals practice and participate. They research background information, statistics, ratings, and personal interest information to provide the audience with the most thorough and interesting coverage of each sports event.

News anchors specialize in presenting the news to the listening or viewing public. They report the facts and may sometimes be asked to provide editorial commentary. They may write their own scripts or rely on the station's writing team to write the script which they then read over the TelePrompTer.

Again, research is important to each news story and the news anchors should be well-informed about each story they cover as well as those they simply introduce. Some news anchors specialize in certain aspects of the news such as health, economics, politics, or community affairs.

For television anchorpeople, research, writing, and presenting the news is only part of the job. Wardrobe, make-up, and presentation also need to be focused on, and getting physically ready for the day is an important part of the job. Many details such as which hairstyles and which outfits to wear are important to create an effective look for the news.

The Internet and the World Wide Web are changing the job of anchorpeople in radio and television. Many radio and television stations have their own Web sites where listeners and viewers can keep updated on current stories, email in comments and suggestions, and even interact with the anchors and reporters. Also, the World Wide Web has become another resource for anchors as they research their stories.

Because their voices and faces are heard and seen by the public on a daily basis, many radio and television anchorpeople become well-known public personalities. This means that they are often asked to participate in community activities and other public events.

What Is It Like to Be an Anchor?

While some may think that being a television anchorperson is a glamorous job, Lis Daily offers an analogy that puts that myth to rest. "It's like doing a term paper every day," says Lis who has worked as a reporter, anchor, and now community affairs director at WTHR, the Indianapolis-based NBC affiliate.

The time an anchor's day begins depends on which newscasts they work on. For an anchor who works during the evening news slots, the day begins about 2:00 PM. Before even coming into the station, the anchor should, Lis says, "at the very least, read the paper."

Once the workday begins, Lis checks the board for what stories are currently being worked on and assigned, and reads the wire services for current news information. The producers, writers, and anchors then meet to look at the lineup and plan the day's news coverage.

"When I worked as an anchor, I always communicated with the reporters about each story we were covering," says Lis. This communication gives the anchor an understanding of the subject and the story, so if the live

What Is It Like to Be A . . . ?, CONTINUED

shot dies or more information is needed, Lis could talk with the reporters on the air or capsulize the story, if needed.

Often, four hours of research and preparation translates into just one and a half minutes of air time, so good, concise writing is important. As an anchor, Lis writes some of her own scripts and stories and relies on the writing team to provide others. Of course, before going on the air, anchorpeople read the entire newscast to prepare themselves for the broadcast. "You must appear confident and credible during each story that is presented," says Lis. The keys to that confidence and credibility are research, preparation, and poise.

> **"You must appear confident and credible during each story that is presented."**

The WTHR-TV Web site is available to viewers twenty-four hours a day, and many of the viewers send email messages and keep updated on current news. This, combined with a 13-Listens program where Lis and another anchor conduct public forums in different areas of the city, keeps the newsroom in touch with the viewing public. As a well-known, on-air personality and community affairs director, Lis often attends community events as a representative of the station.

"I think we're moving toward a more civic journalism," says Lis. "We try to be in touch with the real people who watch us and what their concerns are." Lis and the news team she works with have found that issues such as education and where the Indiana lottery money is being spent are important to their viewers.

Besides being knowledgeable, television news anchors must also look the part. Meeting with clothing consultants, having makeup done, and paying careful attention to physical appearance are all part of the job. Because certain visual effects, like the weather map, are projected onto a blue screen behind the anchors, "you can never wear blue," says Lis with a laugh. "Unless you want the map on you!"

HAVE I GOT WHAT IT TAKES TO BE AN ANCHOR?

Aspiring radio and television anchorpeople must have a mastery of the English language—both written and spoken. Their diction, including correct grammar usage, pronunciation, and no regional dialect, is extremely important. Anchorpeople need to have a pleasing personality and voice, and, in the case of television anchorpeople, they must also have a pleasing appearance.

This emphasis on appearance can be one of the frustrating things about the job. Chris Field, a sports anchor at WTVT, a FOX-owned and -operated station in Tampa Bay, Florida, says, "Sometimes you've put so much effort trying to tell a great story with accuracy and good writing, and then what the viewers remember is how your hair looked that day."

Lis echoes that feeling, "It can be difficult constantly being told how to wear your hair or how to dress." The criticism moves beyond physical appearance at times, but Lis advises, "You can't be all things to all people. Someone once told me to be like a duck—just let it roll off your back."

Anchorpeople must be able to handle deadline pressure and be able to "wing it" or improvise when necessary. "The news comes on at 5:00 PM. If you aren't done, it still goes on," says Lis.

Anchorpeople need to be creative, inquisitive, aggressive, and should know how to meet and interact with people. "Building a network of people and news sources is important," says Lis. "Then those people call *you* when they have their next news tip."

Lis' favorite part of her job is when she is able to make a difference in people's lives. "I think our job is to inform *and* assist whenever we can," says Lis. For example, the station Lis works at sponsors a "Thursday's Child" segment that highlights children who need adoption, a foster home, or just a big brother or sister. With an 80 percent success rate of bringing people together, it is one of the visible ways Lis can see that she is making a difference.

To be a successful radio or television anchorperson, you should:

- Be able to handle deadline pressure and be able to "wing it" or improvise when necessary
- Have a mastery of the English language, including good diction, correct grammar usage, and pronunciation
- Have a pleasant speaking voice, and if on television, a professional appearance
- Be creative, curious, and aggressive—yet know how to meet and interact with people in a friendly manner

How Do I Become a Radio or Television Anchor?

Education

High School

In high school, you should focus on a college preparatory curriculum, according to Steve Bell, a professor of telecommunications at Ball State University. A former network anchor who now teaches broadcast journalism, he says, "One trend that concerns me is that some high schools are developing elaborate radio and television journalism programs that take up large chunks of academic time, and I think that is getting the cart before the horse. There's nothing wrong with one broadcast journalism course or extracurricular activities, but not at the expense of academic hours."

In that college preparatory curriculum, you should learn how to write and use the English language in literature and communication classes. Subjects such as history, government, economics, and a foreign language are also important.

"If you want to be a broadcast journalist, start with learning to be a journalist," says Bell. "Be someone who knows and understands what's going on in the world."

Even at the high school level, Lis advises exploring opportunities to work during the summers at local radio or television stations or to job-shadow an anchor or reporter for a day. "It's never too soon to get your foot in the door," she says.

Top Markets

The television markets are ranked by Nielsen, and television anchors interested in moving up always know the number of the station where they would like to work. The top 25 markets are

1. New York, NY
2. Los Angeles, CA
3. Chicago, IL
4. Philadelphia, PA
5. San Francisco–Oakland–San Jose, CA
6. Boston, MA
7. Washington, DC
8. Dallas-Ft. Worth, TX
9. Detroit, MI
10. Atlanta, GA
11. Houston, TX
12. Seattle-Tacoma, WA
13. Cleveland, OH
14. Minneapolis, MN
15. Tampa–St. Petersburg–Sarasota, FL
16. Miami–Ft. Lauderdale, FL
17. Phoenix, AZ
18. Denver, CO
19. Pittsburgh, PA
20. St. Louis, MO
21. Sacramento-Stockton-Modesto, CA
22. Orlando–Daytona Beach–Melbourne, FL
23. Baltimore, MD
24. Indianapolis, IN
25. Portland, OR

Postsecondary Training

When it comes to college, having your focus in the right place is essential, according to Professor Bell. "You want to be sure you're going to a college or university that has a strong program in broadcast journalism, where they also put a strong emphasis on the liberal arts core."

Some advocate a more vocational type of training in preparation for broadcast journalism, but Bell cautions against strictly vocational training. "The ultimate purpose of college is to have more of an education than you have from a trade school. It is important to obtain a broad-based understanding of the world we live in, especially if your career goal is to become an anchor."

> *"Volunteer if you have to. I have a friend who started in the mail room and now is a news director in Pittsburgh."*

A strong liberal arts background with emphasis in journalism, English, political science, or economics is advised, as well as a telecommunications or communications major.

Lis even advises obtaining a degree with strong emphasis in another field, such as her college emphasis in telecommunications and chemistry. Chris Field's liberal arts degree included two majors—communications and biology. In both cases, some of their first jobs were reporting on health- and science-related issues.

Internships and Volunteerships

Bell also advises participation in extracurricular activities and an internship. "Internships are becoming more and more important. There are so many people trying to get in at the entry-level that you need to have that experience."

Chris Field agrees that internships are important to the college student. "Internships are critical. Do as many as you can in news and production. Knowing how things run behind the camera, how to shoot, and even what a director does is important."

Many news anchors get their first jobs directly from their internship assignments, and Bell advises choosing your internships carefully to make sure

How Do I Become A . . . ?, continued

that they offer many opportunities for hands-on experience in writing and editing.

"Volunteer if you have to," says Lis. "I have a friend who started in the mail room and now is a news director in Pittsburgh."

Who Will Hire Me?

Most radio and television news anchors do not begin their careers with that title. They begin as reporters or writers. "You really have to have experience as a reporter to do a good job and have the respect of your colleagues," says Lis.

"At the networks, you find few, if any, anchors who have not put in their time in the field," says Steve Bell, who is a former ABC anchor. "If you look at today's anchors, every one has put in extensive time in the field as a reporter."

One crucial aspect of finding a job is the internship experience. Both Lis Daily and Chris Field began their broadcast careers at the same television stations where they did their internships. Even if your first job is not at the same station, experience counts when job-hunting.

Once you have the college degree and some experience, finding work means sending out tapes and resumes. According to the National Association of Broadcasters (NAB), there are 1,550 broadcast television stations and 11,800 radio stations in the United States. While that may seem like a large market for your job search, the competition for anchor jobs is keen.

The NAB maintains a list of current job and internship openings, and with the boom of cable and satellite television, there are now more stations at which to apply.

Advancement possibilities

Producers plan each aspect of the newscast, from the writing to the direction and set design.

Press secretaries serve as spokespeople for political figures and other celebrities.

News directors supervise on-air "talent," producers, reporters, editors, and other newsroom staff. They decide which news events will be covered and assign staff to gather information and report on them.

Where Can I Go from Here?

Radio and television anchorpeople move up by moving on. In other words, one of the main ways to advance within the industry is to move to a larger market or larger station. Chris Field has a goal of someday working as an anchor at the network level. She began at the same small station where she did her internship, working in production and hosting a talk show. Eventually, she moved to Alabama to work as an anchor/reporter in a small market. She moved up to a station in Tennessee and then to North Carolina, and with her most recent move to Tampa, she is now working in one of the top markets in the country. Like Chris, the ultimate goal of many anchorpeople is to advance to the network level.

And some, like Lis Daily, move into a director position such as her community affairs director position. Lis also worked as the press secretary for former Indiana Attorney General Pam Carter. Some anchorpeople may also move into producer positions.

WHAT ARE SOME RELATED JOBS?

The U.S. Department of Labor classifies radio and television anchorpeople under the heading, Writers. Also under this heading are people who research and write material for performance, publication or broadcast. This includes reporting, analyzing, and interpreting facts, events, and personalities; and developing fiction or nonfiction ideas. They may rewrite material or perform editorial duties but are primarily responsible for originating written material. Related jobs include copy writers, newswriters, continuity writers, technical writers, writers, columnist/commentators, editorial writers, reporters, readers, screenwriters, script readers, critics, humorists, librettists, lyricists, playwrights, and poets.

Related Jobs
Columnist/commentators
Continuity writers
Copy writers
Critics
Editorial writers
Humorists
Librettists
Lyricists
Newswriters
Playwrights
Poets
Readers
Reporters
Screenwriters
Script readers
Technical writers
Writers

WHAT ARE THE SALARY RANGES?

According to a 1996 Salary Survey conducted by the Radio-Television News Directors Association (RTNDA) and Ball State University, salaries for the industry are holding steady. Salaries for radio news anchors are lower than for television news anchors. Also, larger stations and larger markets pay more than smaller stations and smaller markets.

What Are the Salary Ranges?, continued

For radio anchorpeople, salaries range from a low of $10,000 to a high of $85,000 with an average salary of $26,200. For television anchorpeople, salaries range from a low of $14,000 to a high of $400,000+ with an average salary of $54,100. For television anchors in larger markets, salary negotiations might include such extras as a clothing allowance.

"You probably won't make a lot at your first couple of jobs," says Chris Field. "My first anchor job was at a small station. I earned $12,000—I didn't have a television or a microwave, and worked sixteen-hour days. I wouldn't want to do it again, but I'm grateful I had that experience."

What Is the Job Outlook?

Competition for radio and television anchor jobs is high because the number of people who want to become anchors is much greater than the number of jobs available. While small radio stations and television stations are more likely to hire beginners, the pay is low and the hours are long.

Hopeful anchorpeople who have a variety of broadcast experience and expertise in other areas such as business, sports, or health may have an advantage over others. Most openings in the field will occur due to workers leaving the work force or transferring to another field. According to the RTNDA's 1996 Salary Survey, newly created positions at start-up stations are sometimes available, but most of those positions are for producers or behind-the-scenes personnel.

Employment for radio and television anchorpeople is not closely tied to the economy; if economic downturns affect revenues, stations most often cut "behind-the-scenes" people rather than anchors. Even so, the job outlook for radio and television anchor is likely to remain stable, but not experience significant growth, through 2006.

Reporters and Correspondents

SUMMARY

DEFINITION
TV and radio reporters and correspondents *write and record the daily news segments for broadcast. They conduct on-air interviews, edit recorded footage, and report live from remote sites. They may also work as anchors, introducing news segments and reading news briefs to radio and TV audiences.*

ALTERNATIVE JOB TITLES
Broadcast journalist

SALARY RANGE
$15,000 to $30,000 to $150,000+

EDUCATIONAL REQUIREMENTS
Some postsecondary training

CERTIFICATION OR LICENSING
None

EMPLOYMENT OUTLOOK
About as fast as the average

HIGH SCHOOL SUBJECTS
English (writing/literature)
Geography/Social studies
Government
Journalism
Speech

PERSONAL INTERESTS
Broadcasting
Current Events
Film and Television
Photography
Writing

Flames lick the dark sky. Water from hoses guided by firefighters arcs over the house. A family, in tears, stands in the street. Tom Elser, a reporter for KMTV-3 in Omaha, Nebraska, sits in the newsroom and hurries to edit these video images together, laying on his own voice-over; he edits in brief sound bites from interviews with eyewitnesses and firemen. He's careful to remain sensitive to the family's privacy, while also providing the viewing audience with information about the fire and how it started. He uses his natural curiosity to cover all the bases, to ask all the questions. *How did the fire get started? How soon will the fire be contained? Where will the family spend the night? What will they do next?*

With the news package complete and ready for broadcast in a half hour, Tom rushes back to the scene. The fire still smolders, but is under control. The wet street reflects the streetlights and the faces of worried neighbors up and down the block. Tom listens to his earphone, and stands before the camera, poised and ready to go live with the report.

49

What Does a Reporter Do?

You're a reporter and you hear a rumor. Something about a corrupt politician, a casino, dirty money. Something about cops on the payroll, a suspicious suicide, some convict's loose lips. What do you do? It's almost instinctual—you sniff around for information. You make phone calls, then more phone calls, looking for leads. "Do you know anybody who knows anybody . . . ?" You use your contacts, and you call in favors. You accumulate information, studying documents and reports. Then maybe, with camera and microphone in hand, you pay somebody a surprise visit. If you're lucky, your interview subject will spill the beans, or at least sweat heavily and blink a lot. And once you have some cold, hard facts, you can edit the story into a nice news "package" to deliver to the folks watching the 10 o'clock news.

Lingo to Learn

Composition: In photography, the arrangement of subjects and camera angles into a series of shots.

Copy: The text for a news report; information considered printable and newsworthy.

Electronic media: Broadcasting companies that transmit information electronically, such as TV and radio stations, cable networks, and news services.

Sound bite: A brief recorded statement (as by a public figure) broadcast on a radio or TV news program; a brief catchy comment suitable for use as a sound bite.

Wire services: News organizations, such as United Press International and the Associated Press, that provide TV and radio stations with information on the latest news.

Or, it might go *something* like that—your work won't always be so dramatic. You won't always be reporting on scandals, and you won't always have time for the amount of investigation needed to break open a controversial story. There aren't enough reports about shady politicians and corrupt corporations to fill the daily newscasts of the thousands of stations across the country. For every big story, there are several small stories: reports about local businesses, home safety, schools, regional sporting events, and other subjects of interest to your community.

Americans spend more than three hours a day listening to the radio; 70 percent of us rely on TV as our main source of news. With this kind of demand for programming, reporters must work hard to come up with story ideas, quickly gather the information, and report while the information is still news. They work with producers and other reporters to exchange ideas and discuss the most newsworthy concerns. After deciding on the stories for that day's newscasts, the reporters will then pursue leads and gather information. Once they have reliable information, they begin to prepare the news package (the videotaped news segment).

Preparing the package involves videotaping interviews and relevant footage. TV reporters may shoot the footage themselves or bring a camera operator to the scene. Radio reporters also typically work alone on the news scene, though they may be assisted by engineers. It is important for radio and TV reporters to understand the latest video and audio equipment. After taping an interview, the reporter will then review the material and determine which information is most significant to the story, as well as edit the material according to the time allotted for the report. The TV reporter looks for the most interesting quotes from the interview subject, and the most relevant visuals and sounds. Often, reporters go live to the scene; the reporter will then introduce the news segment during the newscast and answer questions from the anchor about the story.

Reporters may have specific areas, or "beats," to cover, such as a police station or city hall. Or they may be assigned specific regions within the viewing area. Though most reporters, particularly in radio, are required to cover all the news stories, some stations and newscasts have reporters who focus on particular subject matters—a reporter may specialize in reports on crime, technology, health care, entertainment, or business. Most reporters only report on that day's news, but, in some cases, a reporter may spend several days with a particular news story, such as on a news magazine program. An investigative report might also be broadcast as a series within a daily newscast.

The three major networks (ABC, CBS, and NBC) offer daily news coverage of events of national interest; there are also cable channels (such as CNN and MSNBC) that provide around-the-clock news information. With bureaus in Washington, DC, New York, London, and other cities, the networks provide job opportunities for many reporters. These positions are highly competitive, however; most broadcast reporters work in cities all across the country for network affiliates, local cable news channels, or radio news stations.

What Is It Like to Be a Reporter?

Susan Kopen Katcef is a reporter/news anchor for WBAL-AM Radio, a news/talk station in Baltimore. "I'm a clock watcher," she says, describing the nature of a reporter. "I'm acutely aware of every minute of the day." When she's out on the news scene covering a story, her mind is fully occupied with the amount of work a good, complete news story requires. "There's so much to do," she says. "I have to think about the person I'm interviewing, the technical details, the other stories I'm working on." And even after carefully preparing a story for broadcast, she may be required to toss the whole project aside to cover a more important, late-breaking story.

What Is It Like to Be A . . . ?, CONTINUED

In the station's newsroom, Susan prepares for going on location by making phone calls, locating interview subjects, and arranging meetings. She also anchors the news, broadcasting live reports on alternating hours. While anchoring, she does live on-air interviews, and takes calls from reporters. "In radio," she says, "we have to be knowledgeable of local, state, national, and international matters." Radio newspeople also must be knowledgeable about a great deal of technical equipment. Anchoring, Susan operates a reel-to-reel tape recorder, a cartridge machine, and a switcher system with multi-audio. With the switcher system, Susan is able to receive Associated Press news feeds and audio from reporters. "I'm my own engineer," she says. "You have to keep ahead of the learning curve."

This technical expertise is important when reporting, as well. For a radio broadcast, you need recorded voices and quotes. Because she often goes out locally without any backup, she has to have a clear understanding of her recording equipment. "I lost an interview once," she says, "covering the Democratic National Convention." Susan also recalls some technical troubles while preparing a story on betting odds for baseball games. (WBAL is the flagship station for the Baltimore Orioles.) "My microphone didn't work," she says. "As a reporter, you have to be able to troubleshoot. You can't be intimidated by the technical equipment." Usually everything goes as planned for Susan. Once she has the story on tape, she goes back to the station to edit it. She picks out sound bites, then logs them in to the switcher for later broadcast.

> **"There's so much to do. I have to think about the person I'm interviewing, the technical details, the other stories I'm working on."**

Tom Elser, a TV reporter for KMTV-3 in Omaha, prepares his reports for the 10:00 PM broadcast. He works Saturday through Wednesday, from 1:30 PM to 10:30 PM (unless late-breaking news keeps him working into the night). The first fifteen minutes of his workday involve reading up on the day's news—consulting the Associated Press wire, newspapers, and earlier newscasts. This is followed by a 1:45 PM meeting with everyone—producers, reporters, writers—involved in that evening's broadcast. They brainstorm ideas, and discuss the most important story possibilities. "I step out of the meeting frequently," Tom

Moments in broadcast reporting history
—May 6, 1937, Lakehurst, New Jersey

Reporter Herb Morrison was covering the mooring of the Hindenberg (an early passenger zeppelin) for later radio broadcast. Though expecting to do simple coverage of the landing, Morrison watched and reported as the Hindenberg burst into flames, creating one of the most famous radio broadcasts in history.

explains, "to make phone calls, checking out the possibility of doing particular stories for that night's newscast." By the end of the meeting, the news staff has decided which stories to cover, and Tom goes to work.

"I spend most of the time on the phone," Tom says. "The hardest part is getting interviews." In his experience, he has realized that compassion is important in working with people, particularly those who have suffered a tragedy. Tom recalls an early story in his career, talking to the family of a murder victim on the day of the crime. "You have to detach yourself from the tragedy," he explains. "You want to comfort them, but you have to ask them questions."

After taping interviews on the news site, along with a cameraperson, Tom then returns to the station to go over the videotape. "I look at the video to determine the best way to tell the story," Tom says. He works with the cameraperson to determine the most compelling footage. "He might suggest using a good, natural sound—like emphasizing the sound of the river." After making these decisions, Tom edits the piece. "And I'm making changes right up until the last minute," he says. But he must allow for about a half hour before the newscast to reach the remote location to go live.

HAVE I GOT WHAT IT TAKES TO BE A REPORTER?

Reporters are level-headed and able to keep calm in stressful situations. In most situations, reporters going live are required to think on their feet. Reporters must also have a good understanding of topical issues, history, geography, and government. And reporters must write and speak well.

Susan stresses the importance of a reporter's desire to learn. "You have to learn quickly," she says, "and respond quickly. And you should also ask straightforward, to-the-point questions." Assertiveness is also important in getting the interview and the answers to your questions. "You can't be a wallflower in the line of duty."

Tom's curiosity helps him in his work. "I like to know things right when they're happening," he says. "I want to meet people and talk to them. I'm not shy." This helps him to get the interviews he needs. "It can be difficult getting people to talk," he says. "People have become very media-shy."

Have I Got What It Takes?, continued

To be a successful reporter or correspondent, you should:

- Be level-headed and able to remain calm during stressful situations
- Have a strong knowledge of current events, history, geography, and the workings of each level of government
- Have good writing and speaking skills
- Be curious about the world around you and willing to learn
- Be assertive and able to ask direct, straight-to-the-point questions
- Be ready to travel and work odd hours, including holidays and weekends

Both Tom and Susan appreciate being eyewitnesses to history. Susan has had opportunities to travel; she's covered the opening of the Epcot Center, and in 1996, she attended the presidential inauguration. Despite her experience as a reporter, Susan still must work weekends. "As a reporter," she warns, "your life is not entirely your own." You may also be required to move to take other jobs.

Tom would prefer better work hours, as well. "You work all holidays," he says. "All weekends." He would also prefer more time to prepare stories. "The work is highly intense," he says. "I'm kind of a perfectionist, but I only really have time to make the report presentable. I don't always have time to get it exactly the way I want it."

How Do I Become a Reporter?

Susan and Tom both became interested in journalism while in high school, went on to broadcast journalism schools after graduation, and pursued internships. Tom interned as a producer for a morning show broadcast, then went on to KMTV-3. Susan had many internships, and worked on the college radio station where she made connections in the business. During her senior year of college, she worked as broadcast manager for the radio station, took twelve credit hours, worked weekends for the ABC radio station in Washington, DC, and interned four days a week at WBAL radio.

Education

High School

You should take courses in journalism, English, history, geography, and political science. Working for your high school newspaper or radio station will provide you with valuable experience interviewing, editing, and writing. Try out for a speech team to hone your speaking, debating, and research skills. Also, become familiar with video and recording equipment by working for your high school's media department. You may be able to find part-time work or internships with smaller radio and TV stations or newspapers. Contact a local reporter and ask to spend a few days shadowing him or her to get a sense of the work involved.

Postsecondary Education

Reporters can sometimes find work without a journalism degree, but a good school can provide you with professional contacts and internship opportunities. Some students even pursue master's degrees in journalism. Broadcast programs require students to take courses like reporting, photography, ethics, and broadcast history. Many schools also have TV and radio stations that either employ students or offer students credit for their work. The Accrediting Council on Education in Journalism and Mass Communications (ACEJMC) can provide you with information on journalism schools. A list of the Web pages of some of the journalism schools across the country is found at http://www.sscf.ucsb.edu/~hanterm/j-schools.htm.

Internships and Volunteerships

Your college journalism program will direct you to internship programs. Some colleges bring in recruiters from the networks, and from TV and radio stations in major markets. Paid internships with TV and radio stations are highly competitive, but they're also the most valuable. Unpaid interns are restricted to the amount of work they are allowed to do for a station, and therefore receive only limited experience. Some internships may be available in your local area, and others will require you to move; internships are also advertised in newspapers and on Web pages, and listed with various professional organizations. The Society of Professional Journalists offers some annual internship opportunities. A list of many internships, along with job listings, can be found at http://www.tvjobs. The Minorities in Broadcasting Training Program (http://www.webcom.com/mibtp/) provides opportunities for college graduates with journalism backgrounds to train as radio or TV reporters.

Labor Unions

In most smaller markets, reporters aren't required to belong to the American Federation of Television and Radio Artists (AFTRA); the networks and the TV and radio stations in larger cities do require union membership. AFTRA, comprising dues-paying actors, announcers, DJs, newscasters, editors, writers, directors, and vocalists, has seventy-seven thousand members across the country. The union acts as an advocate for better wages, working conditions, and benefits. It isn't necessary to join AFTRA until you have hired on with a station that requires membership.

WHO WILL HIRE ME?

Experienced reporters are in demand throughout the country, in small markets and large. Positions are usually advertised in the local newspapers, or on the job lines of broadcast stations. You may have to submit tapes of your work along with a resume; you should also be persistent in getting your work reviewed for consideration. By doing an on-line search of broadcasting job listings, you're likely to bring up a number of Web sites with descriptions of available positions.

Susan considers herself lucky that she's been able to stay in the same area, despite having changed jobs several times. Susan made many connections while working as a reporter in college. An internship led to work for a Baltimore radio station. She left to work for a Baltimore TV station, but after realizing her preference for radio reporting, quit TV after six months to return to the radio station. "By then," she says, "they had changed to an all-news format. They then changed formats again, and everyone lost their jobs." Susan then worked for a short time as a press/legislative aide before returning to broadcasting as a TV reporter/producer for Maryland Public TV. During the last few years of her five-year stint with public TV, Susan also worked part-time for WBAL radio in Baltimore. She eventually hired on full-time, and has been with WBAL for five years.

Tom's internship also led to full-time work, but only after he left the Omaha station for a CBS affiliate in nearby Lincoln. As a regional reporter, Tom covered the news within one-hundred miles of the city. "There I shot the stories and edited them," Tom says. "Now I work with a photographer." After eight months as a regional reporter, Tom returned to KMTV-3 in Omaha.

Advancement possibilities

News anchors host newscasts on television and radio. They read news copy and introduce live and taped news segments.

Foreign correspondents are reporters who live abroad and report on international stories, events, and cultural issues that are of interest to home viewers and listeners.

Station managers oversee the daily operation of radio and television stations. They supervise all the station departments, such as sales and marketing, management, technical, and on-air "talent."

WHERE CAN I GO FROM HERE?

"I've had so many life changes," Susan says, "that I gave up years ago making plans." But she does have some ideas in mind for her future with broadcasting. "I would like to work on a broader scope." After spending three weeks recently in China as part of a journalist exchange program, Susan became interested in the future of journalism. She would like to work for an organization like

Freedom Forum that promotes fairness in the media, helping journalists develop a better understanding of ethical issues.

Though Tom enjoys reporting, he would eventually like to move into the promotions department, or some other area of broadcasting. "I mostly enjoy the writing and video," he says. "But it wouldn't have to be reporting."

For those willing to relocate, advancement means moving up into a larger market, or into network news. Within a local TV or radio station, a reporter may eventually move on to another area of broadcasting, such as directing or producing a newscast. Reporters also become anchors, who are better-paid and more prominent in the newscast. Many more people are employed in sales, promotion, and planning than are employed in reporting and anchoring; and people in sales and management positions often draw a better salary than the journalists.

What Are Some Related Jobs?

The U.S. Department of Labor classifies reporters and correspondents under the heading, Occupations in Writing (DOT). Other careers listed under this heading include technical writers, newswriters, screenwriters, fiction and poetry writers, playwrights, editorial writers, copy writers, columnists/commentators, and newspaper reporters. Other careers that require strong oral or written communication skills include interpreters, news directors, disc jockeys, editors, producers, sportscasters, weather forecasters, and traffic reporters.

What Are the Salary Ranges?

As with any broadcasting position, the salary for a reporter varies according to the size of the TV or radio station, the size of the audience, and the reporter's experience. Some reporters in the country make less than $10,000 a year, while some star reporters in major markets may be able to demand over $150,000 (though such salaries for reporters are rare). It may surprise you to know that newspaper reporters, despite less visibility, generally make more money than radio and TV reporters.

Related Jobs
Columnists/commentators
Copy writers
Disc jockeys
Editorial writers
Editors
Fiction and poetry writers
Interpreters
News directors
Newspaper reporters
Newswriters
Playwrights
Producers
Screenwriters
Sportscasters
Technical writers
Traffic reporters
Weather forecasters

What Are the Salary Ranges?, continued

Though TV newscasts may draw larger audiences than radio newscasts, TV reporters make about the same salary as radio reporters. Beginning pay for reporters in small markets can be as low as some of the lowest-paying positions in any profession. With yearly salaries of less than $15,000, many reporters strive for the much-higher-paid position of anchor. Even in the smallest markets, anchors make an average of over $30,000 a year. In the top twenty-five affiliates, TV anchors may make close to $150,000 annually (and some star anchors in major markets make much more). In these same top markets, a TV reporter makes only around $50,000 a year.

What Is the Job Outlook?

Newsrooms provide TV stations with healthy profits every year, and this is not expected to change. TV reporters will continue to be in demand; the number of news departments and news staff is expected to increase at a steady rate. But the number of students graduating from broadcast journalism departments is also growing. There are currently over two hundred broadcast journalism programs in the country, and their students don't account for all the reporters seeking work in broadcasting; because news directors hire graduates from many different programs (and some *prefer* to hire graduates with a liberal arts degree), there's growing competition for the available positions.

Salaries are likely to stay low for broadcast reporters. With the large number of applicants for reporting positions, news directors can have their choice of the best without having to pay much. News directors are still not entirely happy with the graduates of broadcast journalism programs—studies done by such organizations as The Society of Professional Journalists and The Freedom Forum report that news directors believe today's reporters can't write well and don't have sufficient understanding of current affairs, history, and geography. Studies such as these may result in radical changes in journalism education, and also in news department hiring practices.

Technology has a big impact on the way news is reported. The development of satellite technology and portable video cameras have revolutionized broadcast journalism over the last twenty years, and new developments over the next twenty years will likely have the same powerful effects. As the Internet competes for TV's viewers and radio's listeners, look for newsrooms to make better use of the technology. Already, many radio stations are broadcasting over the Web, and many TV stations have Web pages that feature up-to-the-minute local news coverage.

Screenwriter

SUMMARY

DEFINITION
Using dialogue, images, and narration, screenwriters write scripts for dramas, comedies, documentaries, adaptations, and educational programs. They may write complete original scripts, or work on assignment by a producer or director. Screenwriters either work freelance or as part of a staff of writers.

ALTERNATIVE JOB TITLES
Scriptwriter
Staff writer
Story editor

SALARY RANGE
$20,000 to $84,608 to $200,000

EDUCATIONAL REQUIREMENTS
High school diploma

CERTIFICATION OR LICENSING
None

EMPLOYMENT OUTLOOK
About as fast as the average

HIGH SCHOOL SUBJECTS
English (writing/literature)
History
Journalism
Theater

PERSONAL INTERESTS
Entertaining/Performing
Photography
Reading/Books
Selling/Making a deal

On the set of the TV Western "Dead Man's Gun," writer Jeff Cohen watches as his script come to life. Canada of the late-1990s serves as the American Wild West of over one hundred years earlier. Actors in prairie dusters and cowboy hats wait for their cues; a make-up artist touches up the lipstick of an actress in a long, red satin dress. Sitting on the steps of a fake saloon, Jeff discusses the interpretation of a scene with a director. The character, as written, would be more frightened entering the gunfight, Jeff explains. The director takes Jeff's ideas into consideration, then steps up to the camera.

After a few words with the actor, the director begins to shoot the scene. Jeff stays in the background, paying close attention to how the scene fits the concept he created. The gun shakes in the actor's hand; his gun fires blanks, and a man falls to the ground. The actor then drops his gun into the dirt, a gesture that Jeff hadn't written into the script. But the gesture seems perfect. With this satisfying collaboration between writer, director, and actor, the scene is complete.

WHAT DOES A SCREENWRITER DO?

Suppose you have an idea for a science fiction TV movie—your movie, set in the not-so-distant future, concerns green Martians. With a powerful telescope, the U.S. government has been watching these green Martians plowing the red

What Does a Screenwriter Do?, continued

dust of their planet for several years; then one day, without warning, the green Martians turn a shade of purple, a kind of pale fuchsia, and the world panics. You tell your friends about your brilliant idea for a TV movie—they all think it's stupid, but you don't care. You think it's brilliant. This confidence and love for your work, and your fearlessness in the face of rejection, are possibly your most important assets in your career as a writer for television.

Your idea for a TV-movie will, if you're lucky, be the first step in a long trek to seeing the show on the air. Because not only must you be good at characterization, plot, writing dialogue, and the many other techniques of storytelling, but you must also be a good salesperson—you'll be expected to represent your work, defend, and promote it. And although the idea formed in the privacy of your own head, you'll be collaborating on the movie with many professionals. Depending on your involvement with the project, you may be working directly with producers, directors, editors, and other writers. You may be required to be on the set during filming, and you may be expected to make revisions at the drop of a hat. And if the movie is being filmed by a small production team, you may be involved in casting, finding locations, and even promoting the film.

So, you have your purple Martian idea. What's next? There are various ways that writers get their work produced. Some writers compose entire scripts, sitting alone in their homes with their computers. They pay close attention to the elements of the story, developing interesting characters and situations. They come up with the lines the characters will say to each other. All of this requires not just talent, but an understanding of how a story moves forward. Writers gain this understanding by watching movies and TV shows, and reading short stories and novels. They also read published scripts of well-written films. In composing your Martian script, you must also format it properly, with proper spacing for cues, directions, and spoken lines.

Then comes the next step: selling the script. This can be the most frustrating and difficult aspect of writing for television. Thousands of people are

Lingo to Learn

Agent: A person with connections in the industry; for a percentage of the final sale of a script, an agent will represent a writer, showing the script to producers and directors.

Draft: A complete written script, either revised or unrevised. A "rough" draft is an initial version of a script; a "final" draft is a script ready for production.

Pitch: A description of an idea, usually verbal, presented to a producer or director. A writer pitches screenplay ideas hoping to be hired to write the entire script.

Reader: An entry-level position in a production company; a reader reads through scripts submitted to the company, analyzes them, and determines which are worthy of being passed on to producers.

Treatment: A written proposal for a script; between three and fifteen pages. A treatment offers a plot summary.

trying to sell their scripts to TV and the movies. Selling your script requires a contact within the TV industry. Some writers have many connections with producers and directors; they've gained these connections by living in Los Angeles, the base for television production. These writers promote themselves and their work. They may take entry-level jobs with production companies and get to know the people who make decisions on scripts. Many writers also have agents; for a percentage of the money you make from the script, an agent will use his or her connections in the industry to get the script read and considered for production. But the services of an agent can be as difficult to obtain as a reading by a producer. And even if you do sell your Martian script, there's no guarantee that the script will ever be produced. Some writers have made whole careers from selling their ideas and treatments for films that ultimately are never made.

Or maybe you think your Martian story would make for a good episode of a science fiction TV series. If you've established yourself in the industry, and have made valuable connections, you can get meetings with producers. Even without a fully written script in hand, you can "pitch" your ideas. With a complete understanding of the series and its characters, you can describe your idea to the producer; but be prepared to have other ideas, in case the producer doesn't like the first one. Most network TV series have writing staffs, as well. As a staff writer for a series, you're expected to work long hours, and to collaborate with the other writers, the producers, directors, and actors. Writers for daytime soap operas are often the most diligent of all TV writers—a new episode of a soap airs every day, even in the summer when other series writers can take a break.

OK . . . so maybe you've convinced yourself that the purple Martian idea *is* a bad one. Dramatic television isn't the only outlet for TV writers. Practically everything that airs on network TV or cable starts with a written script. Documentaries, sitcoms, newscasts, and educational programs are just some of the television projects that require the work of writers. And not all writers work in Los Angeles; freelance screenwriters can be found all across the country. TV series are frequently filmed outside of LA, so even series staff writers are finding themselves in New York, Canada, and even Baltimore. And with the number of new cable channels developing with headquarters in various cities across the country, writers can make successful careers outside of LA and apart from the networks.

What Is It Like to Be a Screenwriter?

Jane Barnes is one of these screenwriters living outside of LA. From her office in Normal, Illinois, Jane has written dramatic adaptations of novels, original dramas, and award-winning documentaries. She has also published two novels and many short stories. Working with director Helen Whitney, who lives in New York, Jane has had the opportunity to collaborate on many television projects. Now working on a PBS "Frontline" piece on the Pope, Jane has just returned from a trip to Rome where she spoke to journalists about her subject. "We didn't approach the Vatican," Jane says. "We were elegantly distanced from the Pope." Though she has no intention of interviewing the Pope, she has discovered that even the people who have access to him are unwilling to talk. Such obstacles—uncooperative subjects, unrevealing interviews—are common for the documentary writer. This time, for Jane, it merely means a later, PBS-paid trip to Rome.

Though not every project allows for world travel, Jane does spend a fair amount of time in New York—particularly while working on a recent profile for PBS' "American Masters" series. The project was called "Darkness and Light" and was about fashion and celebrity photographer Richard Avedon. Before the project began, Jane had a hand in writing the treatment, or the proposal, to present to PBS. Once the proposal was accepted, the work began. "The work required in writing a documentary varies," Jane says. Some documentaries require a great deal of scripting. Often a separate writer is brought in to compose the narration for the film, usually someone who is an expert on the subject. But for the Avedon piece, the director wanted as little narration as possible; she wanted the people interviewed within the film to tell the story. The film editor was also involved in the writing, working with the director to shape the film visually.

Documentaries have a "pre-interview" stage, when the director and writers interview the subjects off-camera in preparation for the on-camera interviews. "Pre-interviews have input into how interviews are developed," Jane explains. Even an interview can be a collaboration between writer and subject. "With the questions asked, you shape the interview to get at your point. You get them to say what you want them to say."

Jane must also take time into consideration when composing narration for the final script. "I had ten seconds to describe the history of photography," she says, referring to the small amount of time allotted for that particular segment. But time limitations can be very good for a documentary—it requires a writer to be succinct and specific. "I've even given it as a writing exercise to students in a composition class," she says.

Jane's involvement with the production wasn't limited to writing. She received credit as co-writer and associate producer, and was actively involved in scouting locations. One segment of the documentary was to be filmed in Dallas; the filmmakers were to capture Avedon's reunion with some of the subjects in his book *The American West*. Jane contacted a location scout in Dallas who directed her to various locations, informed her about how to get permission from the city to film, how to clear areas for filming, and other details.

Jane also made an exciting and unexpected discovery in her scouting—the owner of a diner where they were to film was a good friend of Marina Oswald, the widow of alleged JFK assassin Lee Harvey Oswald. Keeping in mind that Richard Avedon frequently chose public and historical figures as subjects, Jane quickly tried to arrange a meeting between Oswald and the photographer, thinking it would make good material for the documentary. "But Avedon passed on the idea," Jane says, emphasizing how a documentary script is a collaboration of not just writer and director, but subject, as well.

Fictional subjects are perhaps just as difficult to control for a screenwriter, as Jeff Cohen might attest. Jeff is the executive story editor for "Dead Man's Gun" an acclaimed Western series on Showtime. His job is to oversee the writing of the episodes, but this sometimes means doing a great deal of the scripting himself. For the series, freelance writers are commissioned to write an episode; these initial scripts, or "drafts" are then submitted to the story department. To get a final draft, some scripts may simply require some polishing up, while others may require a total rewrite. "Sometimes we'll take the germ of an idea," Jeff says, "and rewrite the whole script." A final draft is then sent out to the various other departments—to production, design, casting. As story editor, Jeff then stays with the script through the whole process and is sometimes involved in casting. He works closely with the producer on the set in Vancouver. "I watch what's going on," he says, "and I try to be a help to the director. I might ask the director, 'Is this a love scene, or is he about to be shot?'," Jeff says, in considering, from a writer's perspective, how a scene should be played.

Though freelance writers for "Dead Man's Gun" are paid for each individual episode they write, Jeff is paid on a weekly basis, and is expected on the set from preproduction of an episode to the final shot. The series has received critical acclaim and CableAce award nominations, but there's no certainty that the series will be renewed for another season by Showtime. "It's a dicey business," Jeff says. "At times you're in famine mode, and at other times in feast mode. It's a difficult field and highly competitive."

HAVE I GOT WHAT IT TAKES TO BE A SCREENWRITER?

The competition Jeff speaks of means few jobs for many qualified applicants. Even if you're getting a steady paycheck as a staff writer for a series, you must still be prepared for eventual cancellation of the series. "As a writer," Jeff says, "you never know what your next job will be. From the point of creation of a script to feedback, you wonder if you'll be able to feed your family." And these pressures are in addition to the pressures of creating new and original written work. "You have to pull ideas out of nowhere," Jeff says. "It's all invention."

But a good project, like "Dead Man's Gun," can be invigorating for a writer; a passion for writing is what keeps the TV writer going against all odds. "Research is one of my favorite things to do," Jeff says. "Since I've been writing, I know a lot more about medicine, the law, police work." "Dead Man's Gun" is set in the American West of the nineteenth century, requiring Jeff to become a student of the 1870s. "Now I know what a buckboard [a four-wheeled vehicle that has a floor made of long boards] is," he says, "and I know about powder-based guns, and cartridge-based guns." In addition to his interest in research, Jeff credits his understanding of people, relationships, and psychology as valuable to him in his work. "To be a writer," he says, "you have to have an eclectic background."

Varied interests and curiosity are also important to Jane as a documentary writer. "You have to be flexible in moving from one role to the next," she says. "One day you'll be talking to truckers about where to get a good cup of coffee, then the next day researching the history of photography." And because the process requires a great deal of collaboration, you must be ready to throw away something you just spent a great deal of time writing. "You can't be too attached to the beauty of your own creations," she says.

In addition to the stress caused by the instability of working on a freelance basis, there's a lot of stress in the work itself. "There's more work than you can do," Jane says, "Or more than you can do well. A deadline is a deadline. And you may get an interview, but if you don't get it on film, it's the same as not getting it." Despite these stresses, Jane enjoys the work. "It's fun and interesting," she says. "It's the opposite of being mired in bureaucracy—you get to go for the pulse, for the gusto, in a wonderful way."

To be a successful screenwriter, you should:

- Be able to work on a deadline
- Know how to create vivid characters, scenes, and storylines
- Have strong communication skills
- Have good research skills
- Be aware that no show you create will last forever; you will always need to look ahead to land your next job

How Do I Become a Screenwriter?

After graduating from Sarah Lawrence College, Jane spent many years developing her skills as a writer. She lived for a time in New York City, where she conducted research part-time for a producer/director and for a writer of articles for cooking magazines. She was also writing fiction at the time; on the basis of that work, she was accepted into the Iowa Writers Workshop. An interest in Russia and a trip to Russia resulted in her first novel, *I, Krupskaya,* based on the memoirs of Lenin's widow.

Jeff started out as an actor in high school, then enrolled in a theater program at York University in Toronto. He studied directing and design, and went on to teach acting and voice. He also directed stage plays. "I've never studied writing," he says, "but my acting background has been key in writing dramatic material."

Education

High School

Though talent plays a big part in a writer's success, technical skill is also important. Take English courses that will introduce you to both classic and contemporary works of fiction. In drama and theater courses, you'll learn about dialogue and scenes; you may even have the opportunity to direct a production or to play a role. From these novels and plays, you can pick up the techniques of storytelling. Take any courses that will allow you to hone writing skills, whether with dramatic scenes or short stories. Many schools also have speech and debate teams, as well as journalism departments, that train students in news writing, editorials, research, and writing yearbook copy.

Postsecondary Training

Producers aren't generally interested in a writer's educational background—you'll be judged on your writing and ideas. But film schools do help people make some connections in the industry. These schools will also teach you the basics of filmmaking, and inform you of internships, competitions, and conferences. Many colleges and universities have film departments, but some of the most respected film schools are the University of Southern California, the American Film Institute, and Columbia University. Write to these schools or visit their Web pages for information about course work and faculty.

Most college theater departments offer courses in playwriting, and many English departments are developing undergraduate creative writing programs. In writing workshops, you can develop skills in dramatic and narrative

How Do I Become A . . . ?, continued

structure. There are also many Master of Fine Arts programs in film, theater, and creative writing.

Labor Unions

TV screenwriters are usually required to join the Writers Guild of America (WGA). Members pay $2,500 annually to belong and to take advantage of health care benefits, legal assistance, and payment negotiation. To become a member, you must accumulate a certain amount of writing experience. The WGA publishes a journal called *Written By* and also maintains a very informative Web page (http://www.wga.org) with information on agents, books on screenwriting, research aids, and many interviews with screenwriters.

Who Will Hire Me?

Jane got her first screenwriting work from Helen Whitney, a friend from college who had gone on to become a successful writer/director. Helen read one of Jane's short stories in a magazine and, impressed with her work, invited Jane to collaborate on a project. This has led to many other collaborations, both produced and unproduced. Some of their projects have included a biographical drama about a woman accused of communism during the McCarthy era, and an adaptation of the Willa Cather novel, *The Song of the Lark*. Both projects were awarded by the New York Women in Film, an organization that arranges for dramatic readings of screenplays for audiences of producers and other filmmakers. Another collaboration, a PBS "Frontline" piece on the 1996 presidential campaign, received a Peabody award and an Emmy for best documentary film.

Jeff became involved in writing after moving to California and living in an apartment complex with other writers. He discovered he had a knack for writing screenplay treatments, and returned to Canada where he co-wrote a movie for TBS, then went on to a career as a director and teacher. He also continued to co-write projects, and eventually established himself as a story-editor for Canadian television. He then began writing freelance for episodic TV.

Advancement possibilities

Film writers write scripts for major motion pictures; they may also be called in to revise the scripts of other writers or to write individual scenes.

Producers head productions by arranging for financial backing, as well as bring together creative teams of directors, writers, and actors.

Television directors are in control of the decisions that shape a TV program, and are responsible for a program's overall style and quality.

Jobs as a screenwriter can be extremely hard to come by. "In order to get an agent or a manager," Jeff explains, "you must have a considerable resume." Most established screenwriters credit their own persistence and assertiveness—you should be prepared to work for a while at entry-level jobs with production companies and TV series in order to get to know the people who make decisions on scripts. Of the approximately eight thousand members of the WGA, only a little over half are actually employed, and that's an improvement over previous years. Though we occasionally hear about very young writers and filmmakers, most screenwriters have had to work for years and years in the industry before establishing themselves.

Where Can I Go from Here?

Though Jane will continue to collaborate on projects with director Helen Whitney, she does miss the fiction writing she did earlier in her career. "A novel isn't a collaboration," Jane says, talking about the appeal of fiction writing. "It's your vision. I miss the solitary responsibility. I miss the dreaminess, the woolgathering, getting into the stream of sentences on my own."

Jeff plans to continue with "Dead Man's Gun," should it be picked up for another season. But he also has a feature film script that has been getting him some attention in Hollywood. The script has been read by some of film's best directors and production companies, and is opening many doors for him. "Success as a writer isn't about who you know," Jeff says. "It isn't about luck; it's about what you put on the page. If you have talent, it will be recognized."

Once writers have established themselves in the TV industry, they may move into feature films. But most writers advance within the industry, producing or directing their own projects.

What Are Some Related Jobs?

The U.S. Department of Labor classifies screenwriters under the heading, Occupations in Writing (DOT). Occupations that also fall under this heading include columnists/commentators, copy writers, editorial writers, critics, technical writers,

Related Jobs

Agents

Columnists/commentators

Copy writers

Critics

Directors

Editorial writers

Fiction and poetry writers

Humorists

Lyricists

Newswriters

Playwrights

Producers

Reporters

Script readers

Technical writers

What Are Some Related Jobs?, continued

script readers, fiction and poetry writers, newswriters, reporters, playwrights, lyricists, and humorists. Other related careers include agents, directors, and producers.

What Are the Salary Ranges?

With some TV stars making over a million dollars an episode, many aspiring writers are under the misconception that TV holds big paychecks for them, as well. But TV writers get paid a mere fraction of the salaries of on-screen talent. Those fortunate enough to be among the four thousand employed WGA members had median earnings of $84,608 in 1996. That's still a very good salary, but you have to consider the nature of television—you lose your job when the series is canceled, and many new series don't make it through their first season. But if your series is successful, you can expect to make between $2,000 and $3,000 a week as a staff writer for a successful network drama, plus an additional payment of over $20,000 for every script you write that is actually produced. And if the series continues for several years, and is sold into syndication, you can look to make money from the reruns, as well.

Though TV has 50 percent more jobs for writers than the motion picture industry, writing for TV is not considered steady, reliable work. Many writers work freelance, so they generally can't predict how much money they'll make from one year to the next.

What Is the Job Outlook?

The WGA hopes that 1996's record high for average earnings for screenwriters demonstrates a reinvigorated market after five years of stagnation. Writers will continue to find work with the networks, though the networks are ordering fewer new episodes of prime-time dramas and sitcoms. Viewership for network TV has decreased over the last several years due to competition from cable, videos, and computers. But this competition opens up opportunities for writers. "Dead Man's Gun" is just one of many original series that Showtime has developed, and HBO has won many Emmys and much industry recognition for its original movies and series. Advances in technology may soon allow for two hundred to five hundred cable channels to be piped into your home—screenwriters will be needed to help in the production of programs for these channels.

Sportscaster

SUMMARY

DEFINITION
Sportscasters cover sporting events for radio and TV news; they write, produce, and edit feature segments for broadcast. They anchor newscasts, providing scores and highlights.

ALTERNATIVE JOB TITLES
Play-by-play announcer
Sports anchor
Sports director

SALARY RANGE
$20,000 to $35,000 to $300,000+

EDUCATIONAL REQUIREMENTS
Bachelor's degree

CERTIFICATION OR LICENSING
None

EMPLOYMENT OUTLOOK
About as fast as the average

HIGH SCHOOL SUBJECTS
English (writing/literature)
Health
Journalism
Speech

PERSONAL INTERESTS
Broadcasting
Current Events
Exercise/Personal fitness
Sports
Writing

The squeak of the players' shoes on the floor of the court, the cheering of the crowd. Jeff Spadafora attempts to speak above the noise. He's only allowed a few questions for the interview that will be broadcast live on the evening newscast. He didn't even know until a few minutes ago which player he'd be interviewing. As the engineer sets up the shot, John stands in position. "Three minutes," the engineer says, and John's interview subject is nowhere yet in sight.

But John doesn't worry. He's confident everything will turn out fine. He looks back and becomes involved in the basketball game . . . he's seen hundreds of games, but each new one thrills him. A player makes a drive to the basket and dunks a shot off the dribble—the crowd goes wild, and Jeff's love for the sport alleviates the stress of the live broadcast.

WHAT DOES A SPORTSCASTER DO?

From cricket and squash to cricket squashing, most sports, no matter how unusual, have fans. These fans want information. They want to know scores and stats. They want to hear the play-by-play. They want interviews with sports figures and highlights of recent games. And they also want to learn about the many other aspects of the growing sports industry: sports medicine, fitness, and sports business have become typical subjects for reporters on nightly news programs. Sportscasters, as part of news anchor teams, do more than just sit

What Does a Sportscaster Do?, continued

behind desks and recite the scores of the local high school matches—they are active members of the sports and recreation industry, and of their news team.

If you love sports, then being a sportscaster may be your dream job. You get to know the local players and coaches, and you talk about sports on a daily basis. And you get paid for it. You can also enjoy a certain amount of local or national fame—it's your voice and personality that TV viewers or radio listeners get to know. Some people have made long careers as sportscasters, in cities large and small, and they have become as closely associated with the team as the players themselves. Sportscasters also make live appearances outside of the sports arena to promote their news teams and to get to know their audiences.

A sportscaster for a local network affiliate reports the sports live during news broadcasts—your local news may air two or three times a night. The sportscaster has a few minutes during these broadcasts to announce scores, upcoming sporting events, and to show and narrate highlights from recent games. With a broad knowledge of all kinds of sports, they prepare their segments in the hours before broadcast; they write their scripts, find the most compelling highlights, and time it all to fit within the time allotted by the producer. These sportscasters also record segments for later broadcast—these segments include on-location interviews with various sports figures. They don't just interview the members of local sports teams; they also cover charity sporting events, inspirational sports stories, and report on the business of sports.

Sportscasters on affiliate TV news teams don't do much play-by-play; as a matter-of-fact, they only occasionally report live from sporting events, and then only for a few minutes. To do play-by-play, your best bet may be in radio. Though radio stations employ sportscasters as part of their news teams, stations also need announcers for the live local games they broadcast—usually high school and college games. Sports teams also hire play-by-play announcers. As a member of a team's media relations department, a sportscaster puts together stats and press notes, as well as arranges for interviews to air live during the games. During the actual games, radio sportscasters rely on their knowledge and speaking skills to describe the action to listeners.

Lingo to Learn

Conferences: *In professional and college football, the groups into which teams are divided. (i.e., the NFL is divided into National and American Conferences).*

Division: *In college football, groups of teams, with the first division consisting of the most competitive teams, and the third division the least competitive.*

Franchise: *Enjoying membership in a professional sports league.*

Hat trick: *In a soccer or hockey game, three goals scored by a single player.*

Leagues: *Alliances of sports teams organizing the competitions.*

Yogi-isms

Lawrence "Yogi" Berra, a Hall of Fame catcher for the New York Yankees, has provided the sports media with some of its most amusing and memorable quotes. A term—"yogi-ism"—has evolved to describe a statement in the simple, contradictory style of Yogi Berra's quotes. Here are a few of his own:

—*"You can observe a lot just by watching."*

—*"Baseball is 90 percent mental; the other half is physical."*

—*"If people don't want to come to the ballpark, how are you gonna stop them?"*

—*"If you can't imitate him, don't copy him."*

But the opportunity to do play-by-play isn't limited to radio sportscasters; cable stations in larger cities air live sporting events and rely on the talents of TV sportscasters who either work for the team or the station. National TV sports coverage also calls on the play-by-play skills of network sportscasters. These national sportscasting positions are highly competitive, and often are filled by former professional players; but as more cable channels develop, offering twenty-four hours of sports coverage, more opportunities will open up for sportscasters.

What Is It Like to Be a Sportscaster?

At ABC-affiliate WTEN in Albany, New York, John Spadafora works as the weekend sportscaster, covering all the sporting events. "There are only two on-air sports guys at the station," John says, "so we have to do it all." This means a Wednesday-through-Friday schedule of putting together local feature stories, with anchor duties on the weekend. He usually works 10:00 AM to 6:30 PM during the week, but must remain flexible because of the different schedules of sporting events. "And if there's an important press conference scheduled, I have to be there whatever the time, day or night."

Though most of his feature stories are recorded on tape for later broadcast, he does occasionally go live from events. "I just did a live shot at the local sporting arena last week," he says. "The New York Knicks played an exhibition game there." This live shot involved dealing with the Knicks' public relations staff to set up a brief interview. "I had John Starks on, and just had time to ask him three questions."

John reports on many local sports, including arena football, college hockey, and high school football. He also reports on a local affiliate of the New Jersey Devils hockey team. "All together, depending on the time of year, I go to a couple games a week," he says. "The more people who see you out, the better. That builds your reputation."

WHAT IS IT LIKE TO BE A . . . ?, CONTINUED

Preparing to anchor the 6:00 PM and 11:00 PM weekend sports segments involves determining what to include in the segment and which plays to feature as highlights, as well as writing the script. John must take time into consideration when putting together his show. "I get around five minutes of airtime on the weekend," he says. "If it's a busy news day, I only show maybe one or two plays per game. If it's slow, I can get away with more. If it's an important game, like the Super Bowl, you have to give it more time." After writing for that night's show, the script is put into the computer for John to read off the TelePrompTer during the live broadcast. "And I'm following along on the monitor when we go to the highlights."

During the week, John tapes feature segments. Along with a cameraperson, he goes out on assignment to interview people and report on sports-related subjects. "I'm right in the middle of doing a story on a local woman who's riding in a bike-a-thon across the country," he says. "She's sixty-seven years old, and has asthma. The bike ride is for the American Lung Association. She has to raise $6,000 just to participate. She's an incredible woman." In putting such a piece together, John relies on his creativity. "I'll interview her for about fifteen minutes, but will only use three or four interesting sound bites of about ten to twelve seconds each. I leave the pictures and images up to the photographers [camerapeople]." John stresses the importance of having a good working relationship with the photographers. "I think of it as a team," he says. "We have great photographers and, together, we can usually come up with some really creative shots and an overall way the piece should sound and look."

HAVE I GOT WHAT IT TAKES TO BE A SPORTSCASTER?

The basic requirement for a sportscaster is a love and enthusiasm for sports. Most viewers and listeners of sports news have this enthusiasm and demand it from their sportscasters. These audience members also want someone who is personable and trustworthy, and who can speak clearly and express themselves simply.

John credits his sports knowledge with his success as a sportscaster. "I have a deep knowledge of many sports," he says. "I can remember staying up late on school nights when I was eight years old to listen to the radio and find out how the Yankees were doing on the West Coast." It's this enthusiasm that keeps him interested in his work. "I get to deal with what I love—sports. I get to meet really interesting people in professional and amateur sports." But there is one major drawback to the job—the demand on his time. "There's always news

To be a successful sportscaster, you should:

Be a rabid sports fan

Have confidence in your abilities and never give up when trying to break into the field

Be able to speak clearly and express yourself

Be willing to work at all hours and on holidays and weekends

Be willing to travel

Have a thick skin since fans won't always agree with your opinions or ideas

". . . Christmas, Thanksgiving . . . you can't cut out early one day because you're beat."

Michael advises people pursuing work as a sportscaster to stay confident. "You have to be a go-getter," he says. "I never think that something can't be done." Michael also emphasizes his love for the work. "I get to watch baseball every day. I'm fulfilling a dream." He has had to get used to criticism, however. "After a broadcast, someone might say, 'Why'd you say that on the radio?'" And because the radio broadcast is piped throughout the entire stadium, he sometimes receives this criticism fairly immediately. "But it keeps you sharp," he says. "It keeps you thinking."

How Do I Become a Sportscaster?

John has a dual degree from Syracuse University—in marketing and in television, radio, and film production. While in college, he interned at NBC Sports in New York, working on the 1988 Olympics. "I was in the profile department working on feature pieces. It was incredible to see how much work went into a major production like the Olympics. There were around two hundred pieces produced on athletes, countries, etc."

Education

High School

If you want to be a sportscaster, you need to learn the basics of journalism. In addition to courses that will train you in news writing and reporting, interviewing, editing, and photography, take English composition courses. Physical education courses that offer course instruction in addition to exercise can help you become more familiar with the sports and recreation industry. A health class can teach you about fitness.

Though you may only really be interested in football, baseball, or basketball, to become a sportscaster you should learn about all kinds of sports. Watch ESPN, your local sports news, and read the newspaper's sports page to get to know as much about as many different sports as you can. Go to work for your high school newspaper or radio station, and cover the local sporting

How Do I Become A . . . ?, CONTINUED

events. You may even find part-time work with the sports department of your city newspaper, or with a radio or TV station. Your guidance counselor may be able to direct you to a local mentoring program that could introduce you to professional sports journalists, allowing you the opportunity to shadow a sportscaster for a day or two.

Postsecondary Training

In recent years, broadcast journalism professionals have been debating the value of journalism schools; some believe students should pursue degrees in history and political science for a broader education. Others still stress the importance of journalism school for students wanting careers in broadcasting. Many journalism schools are offering majors in sports journalism, and even graduate sports journalism programs. But the important thing is to gain as much practical experience as you can. Look for part-time jobs with local or college radio and TV stations, and volunteer with sports organizations. Various seminars and conferences are open to college students, including a program sponsored in part by the Churchill Downs. This program invites fifty students of sports journalism to shadow journalists as they report on the trainers and jockeys preparing for the Kentucky Derby.

Advancement possibilities

News anchors host radio and television news broadcasts. They read news copy and introduce live and taped news segments.

Producers supervise the production of newscasts, plan segments, and keep programs running on time.

General managers manage the operations of television and radio stations; they're involved in marketing, promotion, contracts, and public relations.

Internships and Volunteerships

Many TV and radio stations have internship programs, along with summer job opportunities. Most of these internships are unpaid; the paid internships offer better training, but are very competitive. If you're in a broadcast journalism program, your advisers can connect you to available internships; your school may even be visited by recruiters from network and cable sports departments. You can write to the networks for information on their internship opportunities. For example, ESPN offers ten-week internships to college juniors.

Who Will Hire Me?

After graduating from college, John looked locally for work. Channel 10 in Albany happened to have an open position. "I was basically a gofer boy," he says. "I logged tapes and just helped with whatever it took to put the sports segment together." He then started editing all the highlights, and after a year and a half, he was given the opportunity to do a few stories of his own. "They saw that I was motivated and really wanted to be on the air." After another year, John went to work as weekend sports anchor, a job he's had now for about five years.

Some sportscasters get their first paying jobs from the stations for which they intern. TV and radio stations often widely advertise open positions; check your local newspaper for local positions, or consult the Internet for many job listings.

Where Can I Go from Here?

John is presently considering changing jobs. "I'd like to go somewhere that has a professional sports team," he says. "I'm debating whether or not to get an agent. They're helpful, but they take 6 to 10 percent of your contract." John plans to try on his own for a while, using the Internet. Along with his resume, he'll submit a video of his recent work.

Typically, sportscasters start in part-time positions in the smaller markets, then move up into full-time sports anchor positions. They then either advance into a top anchor position or on to a larger market. But many sportscasters work for the same radio or TV station for many years, making successful careers with a local affiliate.

What Are Some Related Jobs?

The U.S. Department of Labor classifies television sportscasters under the heading, Occupations in Entertainment and Recreation, Not Elsewhere Classified (DOT). Other careers that fall under this classification include comedians, television directors, public-address announcers, disc jockeys, and show hosts and hostesses. Related careers that require strong

Related Jobs
Actors
Broadcast meteorologists
Comedians
Disc jockeys
News anchors
Public-address announcers
Public relations workers
Radio and television traffic reporters
Reporters
Show hosts and hostesses
Sportswriters
Teachers
Television directors

oral or written communication skills include interpreters, radio and television traffic reporters, reporters, news anchors, public relations workers, broadcast meteorologists, teachers, actors, sales workers, and sportswriters.

What Are the Salary Ranges?

Salaries vary according to the size of the market and newsroom, and the sportscaster's experience. Though some sportscasters may make the same as news anchors, they typically make less even than weathercasters. Surveys place the median salary for sportscasters in smaller markets at around $20,000. In larger markets, a sportscaster can make nearly $100,000. Most sportscasters make about $35,000, but some star sportscasters in large markets make over $300,000.

What Is the Job Outlook?

Newsrooms provide TV stations with healthy profits every year, and this is not expected to change. Therefore, sportscasters will continue to be in demand, and news staff is expected to increase at a steady rate. But there's a lot of competition for these positions; there are many more graduates of journalism programs than there are jobs. This discrepancy may mean changes in the future of journalism education—look for programs to develop more well-rounded curricula to better prepare students for the workplace.

The ratings for the 1997 World Series were much lower than expected, making TV executives wonder about this decreased audience. Even Monday Night Football, an ABC standby, has suffered some in the ratings. Though baseball fans may still be stinging from the baseball strike, executives don't believe the fans have lost interest in sports—there's just more competition for the networks. The usual suspects—cable, satellite TV, and the Internet—are thought to be taking viewers away. New all-sports cable channels have cropped up alongside ESPN, and more are expected. Though this may be bad news for the networks, it's good news for sportscasters, who will see more jobs available on the national level.

Sportscasters are expanding their area of coverage to include more than sports scores and highlights—their feature stories include reports on the thriving sports and recreation industry, and on health and fitness. The sports segments of newscasts may eventually move toward feature-oriented reports and away from the traditional listing of sports scores and highlights.

Television Director

Summary

Definition
Television directors control the decisions that shape a television program, from live productions and local newscasts to dramatic TV-movies and comedy series. The director is responsible for a broadcast's overall style and quality.

Alternative Job Titles
Producer/director

Salary Range
$28,000 to $50,000 to $120,000+

Educational Requirements
Bachelor's degree

Certification or Licensing
None

Employment Outlook
Faster than the average

High School Subjects
English (writing/literature)
Journalism
Speech

Personal Interests
Broadcasting
Film and Television
Photography
Theater

WWAY-TV, Channel 3, is about to go live with the local news broadcast, and Richard Perry stands in the control booth, wearing a headset. He's listening, and watching, and considering. The camera operator, the anchors, the producer—they're all passing on information from the audio department, and the floor. Looking at the TV screen, Richard prepares to broadcast the first images of that evening's newscast.

Audio gives the countdown, and Richard, with his fingers touching lightly against the controls of the switcher, directs the camera operator. "A two-shot," he calls for, then, smoothly, the TV screen cuts to the two anchors on the set below. With the producer helping him to keep on time, Richard calls for a tape to be rolled, following an over-the-shoulder shot of an anchor and a graphic. After a stressful, fast-paced half hour, the whole day's work of preparing for this one program will be complete. If Richard has made all the cuts and transitions smoothly and clearly, the home audience will remain unaware of all the different elements that go into a broadcast.

What Does a Television Director Do?

Every year, thousands of young directors enlist in the filmmaking departments of schools like UCLA and NYU; others max out their credit cards in hopes of

What Does a Television Director Do?, continued

making low-budget features worthy of the Sundance Film Festival. But there are thousands of directors working who have never been to film school, who don't live in Hollywood, and yet have established themselves in their profession. These people make successful careers and earn regular salaries by directing for network TV affiliates in cities both large and small; or they work for special-interest cable channels, like FoodTV and ESPN; or they work on a freelance basis, taking on a variety of projects for a number of different production companies. Directors work on local news programs, coverage of area sporting events, and commercials for local businesses. And with the development of narrowcasting (broadcasting meant for limited viewing, such as for classrooms, hospitals, or corporations), some directors create programming for very small audiences. Every television project, no matter how short or how small the intended audience, requires a director.

Your duties as a director depend on the nature and size of the project. Whether directing a rock music video or a live presentation of a symphony orchestra, a pay-per-view broadcast of a brutal boxing match or a TV-movie about a famous boxer's life, all directors have one thing in common: they direct the talents and skills of a number of professionals, bringing together all the pieces to create a complete program. The director is responsible for creating the look of a broadcast by determining camera angles and cuts. The director of a TV-movie, documentary, or an episode of a series, will generally have more control over the material and its interpretation than the director of a news broadcast or a live event. If you're directing a movie, you're working from a script, you're rehearsing with the actors, you're shooting and reshooting scenes from many perspectives. To achieve the intended mood and tone of the piece, you carefully organize the work of screenwriters, lighting and sound technicians, camera operators, and editors. But if you're covering a baseball game, you have much less control—you get only one shot at broadcasting that game, leaving little room for error. And with reporters turning in pieces right up until the hour of a news broadcast, TV news directors don't even know the final content of the evening edition until just before it airs.

Lingo to Learn

Clapsticks: The hinged, typically black-and-white, boards "clapped" together at the beginning of a shot.

Editor: A member of a production team who views all the shots filmed by the director and decides which ones to use and how to use them.

Over-the-shoulder: In news production, a shot of an anchor with a graphic above the shoulder; in dramatic production, means a shot from behind someone, literally "over the shoulder."

Two-shot: A shot which features two subjects (such as actors, anchors, reporters) in one frame.

Wipe: An image sliding across another image, as with letters across a screen.

Do you thrive on stress? Are you able to make snap decisions? Do you want to take part in live events and late-breaking news? Events such as the summer and winter Olympics, professional and college football games, and awards presentations require the talent of directors; these directors work with the announcers, the camera operators, and other members of the technical crew to smoothly broadcast a live—and sometimes unpredictable—program. But you don't have to work for a network sports or news department to cover live events. For the director of the local news of a network affiliate, every day requires quick reflexes and focus. As a news director, you're responsible for getting all the news segments on the air; during a broadcast, you sit in the control room giving orders, keeping the broadcast moving smoothly from segment to segment. Wearing a headset, you receive information from the producer and technical crew. The camera operators work from your direction. But the director's job isn't limited to the actual broadcast; you must also direct promotional segments, news updates, and some videotaped segments to accompany the live reports later.

In smaller TV stations, the directors of nightly news programs may be involved in many different aspects of the production. They may create graphics and supers (short for "superimposed" words running across the screen, such as the names of interview subjects, or titles of a news segment), and pie charts and graphs and other informational pieces. In a larger station, the work is divided up among the directors, producers, editors, assistants, and technical directors. (Technical directors are members of the technical crew, who work directly with the cameras and other equipment.)

But maybe you're interested in working with a variety of projects—many directors work freelance. When taking on different projects for different producers, your job description changes frequently. You may work as a director on one project and as technical director on another. You may be directing actors in an original drama, or interviewing people for a documentary. Or you may take on many elements of the production, from getting funding for a project, to hiring writers and assistants, to setting up locations. You may even be involved in publicizing the film and entering the film into festivals and competitions.

What Is It Like to Be a Television Director?

The next time you watch the evening news, pay attention to the camera changes, the words that flash across the screen, and the graphics above the

WHAT IS IT LIKE TO BE A . . . ?, CONTINUED

shoulder of the news anchor. You probably rarely think about all these various elements, unless something goes wrong. It's Richard Perry's job to make sure all the segments of the newscast flow freely together. Richard Perry is a director/editor for WWAY TV-3 in Wilmington, North Carolina. Though he directs the 5:30 PM newscast, he reports for work at 5 AM to help prepare for the morning show, as well as to direct the various updates and promotions to be broadcast throughout the day.

From 5:00 AM to 6:00 AM, he makes the graphics for the morning news, "and I prep the supers." The newsroom sends a printed list of the words and titles, or supers, needed to run across the screen during the broadcast. He types the supers into the chryon (the character generator). From 6:00 AM to 7:00 AM, Richard then runs the chryon for the morning show. This involves hitting the control for running the words across the screen at the right time. From 7:00 AM to 8:30 AM, Richard directs the local weather and news cut-ins for broadcast during "Good Morning, America."

Splitting his shift, Richard then leaves work at 9:00 AM, and doesn't return until 2:00 PM. From 2:00 PM to 4:00 PM, Richard works on commercial production, then begins preproduction for the evening news. "We make graphics for over-the-shoulder shots," Richard explains, "and put boards on tape for the news editors to put in their stories." Boards are graphics and lists of information; these boards are videotaped, then edited by the reporter directly into news packages (or self-contained stories on tape, consisting of the reporter's audio and edited video). In the half hour before the evening news, Richard goes over the script. Then begins the 5:30 PM broadcast—"also known as the half-hour adrenaline rush," says Richard.

Most TV stations have both a director and a technical director—the director calls the shots, and the technical director makes the adjustments on the control board. But in a smaller station like Richard's, directors take on many responsibilities. "I sit in front of the switcher," Richard says, "and tell everyone what to do, and push all the right buttons at the right time so the show looks smooth." He tells the camera people what to shoot next, and calls for tapes to be played, or rolled, during the broadcast.

Pat Lowry also directs live broadcasts as a freelance director in Texas. After working as a producer/director for NASA for four years, she decided to pursue her love for working in televised sports. As a technical director, Pat works NBA games in Texas. But, because freelance work can be unpredictable and insecure, she takes on a variety of projects, including the annual live broadcast of the Miss Texas pageant. She also continues to do consulting work for NASA, and she did videotape work for the volleyball broadcasts of the 1996 Summer Olympics.

While at NASA, Pat produced and directed 250 shows. These educational programs and documentaries included a program about NASA for viewing by President Clinton and Boris Yeltsin in Moscow in 1994. Within 4 years, Pat had worked her way up to managing the NASA TV contract, and had 50 people working for her. "But I wanted to do live TV again," Pat says.

"Directing is quite an undertaking," she says, "dealing with a number of people." The Miss Texas pageant, which is broadcast live across the state to over six million viewers, involves six months of planning for one two-hour period. "It's sink or swim" she says.

Have I Got What It Takes to Be a Television Director?

As a director, you must be prepared for a lot of stress; many people, from producers, newscasters, and camera operators to the actual home audience, are relying on your talents. Because you're working with many different professionals, you must also be good at listening, and capable of incorporating their ideas into the program or live broadcast.

"I'm a pretty good leader," Richard says, describing the skills required of a good director. "You have to be in order to pull together so many people to this one common goal: getting the show on the air cleanly." He also has to make snap decisions when things go wrong. "I have an ability to focus on whatever is before me, and to block out everything else that is unnecessary."

The work takes a lot of self-confidence because you're probably going to be berated from time to time by stressed-out co-workers. "You never know if the producers and directors will be jerks," Pat says. As a thirty-five-year-old woman working in sports, Pat occasionally must deal with the egos of older men. "Barriers are being broken," Pat says, "but there is sexism in sports TV." But Pat is quick to point out that this sexism doesn't exist everywhere; despite the large numbers of men running NASA, Pat had many opportunities to advance. "You have to have a lot of drive and ambition," she says, "and a determination to continue."

Richard also points out the personality conflicts that can arise with producers and

To be a successful television director, you should:

- Be able to handle stress and meet deadlines
- Be a good listener who is able to incorporate the ideas of others into your work
- Be a leader and be able to make intelligent snap decisions
- Be able to handle occasional criticism and second-guessing from viewers and co-workers
- Be ambitious and willing to work very hard to attain success

Have I Got What It Takes?, continued

directors. "We tend to work those things out," he says. "I work with a good group of people." But the most stressful aspect of the job for Richard is the actual newscast. "Sometimes things come in late," he says, "and that causes everything to be reshuffled. It makes for a lot of chaos and it's up to the director to pull it all together."

But both Richard and Pat emphasize the fun of directing. Pat says, "How many jobs allow you to see pro football and basketball games, and get paid for it? Everything you do is an event; people want to see it."

How Do I Become a Television Director?

Richard received a BA in Speech Communications from the University of North Carolina at Wilmington. He got his first opportunity to work in a control room while volunteering for a small cable outfit. He also did video work for a preacher, taping footage at a local prison and other locales. "I learned basic composition of shots then," Richard says.

Pat first pursued an accounting degree when studying at Texas A&M and worked for a video production company. "I started doing four-camera dance recitals and weddings," she says, "and I taught myself how to direct." She then changed her major to broadcast journalism and took a job at the TV station on campus. By the time she graduated she had directed PBS auctions and festivals, and citywide broadcasts.

Education

High School

The sooner you can get to know a camera, and how to set up interesting shots, the better. Pay close attention to the broadcasts and programs you see on TV, thinking about them in terms of camera angles and editing. Work for the high school newspaper and you'll become familiar with reporting and deadlines, and you may have the opportunity to work as staff photographer. Some high schools even have their own TV stations that videotape original programs. Check with your high school's media department about working on the production crews that videotape school events. Plays and presentations are frequently videotaped for the library archives, and tapes of sporting events are used by coaches to review the strengths and weaknesses of the team. If you're less interested in live directing and more interested in working with actors and scripts, get involved with the drama club or the local community theater.

Postsecondary Training

Though a college degree isn't necessarily required of a TV director, it does give you an edge in the workplace. Also, many colleges have internship programs and career services that can help you get your foot in the door, and provide you with directing experience. If you're interested in working for a TV news station, you should apply to the broadcast departments of journalism schools. Some schools require semesters of training; the University of Missouri sends its students to work for a university-owned network affiliate. The students of Northwestern University put together news feeds for a national news service. Contact the Radio-Television News Directors Association (RTNDA) for information on and rankings of broadcast journalism schools.

If you're interested in directing dramas and sitcoms for network and cable TV, you may want to enroll in a drama school to develop a theater background and experience working with scripts and actors. A number of universities and colleges also offer film studies programs. But, no matter what college program you enroll in, one of your top goals should be to develop practical experience. If your college of choice doesn't offer opportunities for learning about cameras and control rooms, you should seek out those opportunities on your own through part-time jobs and volunteerships. Many young directors develop directing skills working for ad agencies, video production companies, and local cable channels.

INTERNSHIPS AND VOLUNTEERSHIPS

An internship with a television news department frequently leads to full-time employment with that same department upon graduation. Because of this, internships can be highly competitive, and many students must take nonpaying internships. The paid internships, however, are the most valuable; federal law limits the amount of work unpaid interns are allowed to do for a station. Only with a paid internship can you get the full experience of working as a director for a TV newscast.

The RTNDA and the Directors Guild of America offer a few fellowships every year. A summer fellowship at the International Radio and Television Society offers an all-expense paid program, which includes career-planning advice and practical experience at a New York-based corporation. They also offer a minority career workshop, which brings students to New York for orientation in electronic media. The DGA-Walt Disney TV Directors Training Program is available for minority and women directors with three years of

How Do I Become A . . . ?, continued

directing experience. This training program involves directors in the production of TV sitcoms.

Labor Unions

Though you can work for a small station without union membership, the networks and major markets require you to be represented by the DGA. The DGA represents film and TV directors, assistant directors, and others. With membership, you'll have access to health care benefits and legal representation. The DGA also offers awards to members and promotes the hiring of minorities and women.

Who Will Hire Me?

Pat developed much of her directing experience while still in college working for a video company and the campus TV station. While working on the Miss Texas pageant, she made a connection that remains valuable for her as a freelance director: she met the head of a production company who hired her to do videotape for NBA games. Her first full-time directing job was for the Texas A&M Sea Grant program. "I produced videos on marine biology, research, and education," Pat says. "I also took photos for their magazine. I learned to dive there so I could do underwater photography and videography." When she learned that NASA was looking for people who could dive and operate underwater cameras, she pursued work with their TV production department.

Richard's internship as a production assistant in his last semester of college led to his permanent position with WWAY-TV. "Honestly," he says, "I never thought I'd be able to direct; it looked so hard . . . so many things going on at once. But I gradually worked my way up through prompter, camera, tapes, audio, and finally I was a director." He worked part-time for the station for three and a half years before being hired on full-time.

If unable to take part in an internship, you can hire on with video production companies or local network affiliates or cable stations. Freelance production companies also offer opportunities for new directors. You should be prepared to take any position that will offer hands-on experience with cameras and production, even if only on a part-time or temporary basis. TV directors are expected to pay their dues in the business and to work hard to learn about all the aspects of the industry.

Where Can I Go from Here?

Pat hopes to have the opportunity to move from technical director to director on TV sports projects. "I had a goal that by the time I was thirty-five," she says, "I would be making a six-figure salary or directing live sports. I've had the salary, but not the chance to direct." She frequently meets some of the best directors in sports TV, and she rarely turns down a project. (Pat has ten different resumes, each one focusing on a specific area of her experience.) But full-time opportunities are tempting her away from freelance. NASA has offered her a management position with a great salary and regular hours.

Though Richard could move into a production manager position, he's happy as director. "If I want to move up as director," he says, "I'll have to move up to a larger market. Maybe Charlotte or Raleigh." Richard advises, "Get in where you can and work your way up. You learn a lot on the way up, and there's a lot of paying of dues in this business." There's not a typical career path for directors, but Richard's advice does define the general sensibility in the television business. Once you've worked on some productions, other opportunities will open up for you.

Advancement possibilities

News anchors oversee news broadcasts. They read reports and introduce other broadcast professionals who specialize in health, investigative reports, weather, or sports.

Film directors oversee the activities of actors and technical staff to create a motion picture.

General managers of television stations supervise sales, personnel, marketing, and technical departments, as well as on-air "talent."

Producers plan and coordinate radio and television broadcasts.

What Are Some Related Jobs?

The U.S. Department of Labor classifies television directors under the heading, Occupations in Entertainment and Recreation, Not Elsewhere Classified (DOT). Other careers that fall under this classification include motion-picture directors, producers, artist-and-repertoire (A & R) managers, stage managers, and radio directors. Related careers in the film and television industries include art directors, assistant directors, casting directors, directors of photography, film editors, screenwriters, and sound editors.

Related Jobs

Artist-and-repertoire managers
Art directors
Assistant directors
Casting directors
Directors of photography
Film editors
Motion-picture directors
Producers
Radio directors
Screenwriters
Sound editors
Stage managers

What Are the Salary Ranges?

Salaries vary greatly and are determined by a number of factors. A director of a newscast of a small TV station may receive very low pay, while a director working for a network can earn tens of thousands of dollars a year. Also, a freelance director working project to project may earn a great deal one year, and much less the following year. Payment for some projects may also involve union negotiation.

The median yearly salary for a director working for a TV station is about $50,000. For news staffs of no more than ten people, a director will make around $28,000 per year; for a larger network affiliate, a director may make up to $120,000 per year.

What Is the Job Outlook?

Despite talk of the Internet taking away from TV's audiences, more TV programs are produced now than ever before, and this number of programs will only grow in leaps and bounds. New technology will allow cable stations to offer hundreds of additional channels and therefore more original programming. Also, more companies and organizations, such as NASA, recognize TV and video productions as ways to educate the public about their work, as well as to train their employees. Directors will be needed for all these projects.

Newsrooms provide TV stations with healthy profits every year, and this is not expected to change. Therefore, directors will continue to be in demand to direct newscasts; the number of news departments and news staff is expected to increase at a steady rate.

Though television has historically been a stepping stone for directors who want to move on to feature films, more directors today are making lifelong careers, with a fair amount of recognition, directing TV. Directors of less-recognized forms like commercials and music videos are beginning to receive more attention: in 1997, for the first time, the Emmy Awards program featured nominations for best TV commercial of the year, and the directors of music videos are now listed along with the performer and record company at the beginning of all videos aired on MTV.

About half of all TV directors work freelance, and that number will likely increase. As TV productions become more costly, and as smaller, less-profitable cable networks produce original programming, hiring directors on a project-to-project basis may be the most economical.

Television Producer

Summary

Definition
Television producers work behind the scenes of television programs and newscasts; they write scripts, hire staff, and bring together the many different elements of production.

Alternative Job Titles
Executive producer
Producer/director
Writer/producer

Salary Range
$17,000 to $40,000 to $200,000+

Educational Requirements
Bachelor's degree

Certification or Licensing
None

Employment Outlook
Faster than the average

High School Subjects
Business
English (writing/literature)
Journalism
Theater

Personal Interests
Broadcasting
Current Events
Photography
Reading/Books
Selling/Making a deal

A train derailment during rush hour in the nation's capitol has injured over one hundred people. As a producer for Newschannel 8, Mike Darnold has twenty minutes to bring the details to his viewing audience. It's been a busy news day and all the stories for the thirty-minute newscast have been determined. He views the outline and the copy he's already written while checking news feeds and taking phone calls. He tries to decide which reports to edit to allow room for this late-breaking event.

Mike has already sent a reporter and a photographer to the scene; on a monitor are the transmitted live images of the train derailment. Mike stays near the phone for information from various sources—he still needs to know the exact number of people injured, and the extent of these injuries. He needs to know the reason for the derailment. He also hurriedly compiles facts and figures—reports from safety records, a history of any previous problems with the train, and other details that can help him produce the most informative newscast in a city where hundreds of reporters compete for the news.

What Does a Television Producer Do?

Since they're involved in writing, editing, budgeting, planning, casting, hiring—and weaving together all the different parts of a production into a complete program, a better question might be, "What *doesn't* a TV producer do?" Producers oversee the production of newscasts, sporting events, dramas, comedies, documentaries, specials, and the many other programs that make up network and cable broadcasting. Because of the varied nature of television programming, a producer's role may also change from project to project. A producer on one project may only be involved in arranging financial backing and putting together the creative team of directors and actors. A producer on another project may oversee practically every detail of the production, including arranging for equipment and scheduling personnel.

Lingo to Learn

AVID: *A brand of a popular computer editing system; allows the editor to edit film on the computer.*

Gaffer: *Working with the grip (the person who maintains the equipment throughout production), the technician who serves as head of the electrical department.*

Postproduction: *Editing, sound, effects, and the other work done on a project after principal photography is completed.*

Shot composition: *How all the elements in a camera shot are arranged, or composed.*

Stock footage: *Segments of film or video kept in a library and reused in various broadcasts.*

Talent: *The on-air personalities who anchor, or narrate, a broadcast. Also, the actors and extras who appear on camera in dramatic productions.*

Maybe your idea of a TV producer has been formed by Nick-at-Nite and its reruns of "The Mary Tyler Moore Show"—Mary and Murray dealing with the on-air antics of Ted Baxter. But a more accurate media portrayal of a producer is by Holly Hunter in the film "Broadcast News." Ambitious, busy, and intelligent, Hunter's character literally runs the show. She comes up with ideas for stories, determines the newsworthiness of events and subjects, chooses graphics, edits taped material, and writes copy. One scene in the film shows Hunter at work during a live newsbreak; she quickly arranges for on-air interviews and organizes information from a variety of sources. She sets up reports from correspondents on the scene. As she speaks softly through a microphone, she directly passes on information to the anchorman through his ear piece, and the film shows us how closely connected she is to the broadcast.

Producers of the daily newscasts across the country are some of the hardest working producers in television. They are required to have great news judgment—along with reporters, they determine which stories are worth broadcasting. They assign stories, review taped reports, and help the reporters edit the material. Paying close attention to time restraints, producers take all the elements of the newscast and piece them together. These pieces include live and taped reports, news feeds, graphics, special segments, and voice-overs. Often producers have to deal with late-breaking developments and must quickly assign reporters and photographers to a story, then weave the new report into the evening's newscast. Producers write scripts for the broadcast from information provided by wire services. The work environment for a TV newscast producer is fast-paced and doesn't let up even at the end of a work day—whenever there's news to be covered, a producer must be prepared to cover it.

Producers for documentaries and specials are also very actively involved in their productions, but they're typically allowed days, rather than hours, to complete projects. They're involved in hiring writers, directors, camera operators, and technicians. They scout out locations and interview potential subjects. With interviews and events on tape, they review the material, select the best footage, and edit it into a program of a pre-determined length. As with a newscast producer, they must also weave in graphics, voice-overs, music, and other effects.

Whereas newscast and documentary producers rely upon their news judgment, producers of dramatic and comedy series rely on their sense of entertainment. They come up with ideas for programs, and hire the talent who can help them execute these ideas. They write scripts from these ideas, or hire freelance writers. And they audition actors and cast them in roles.

What Is It Like to Be a Television Producer?

Mike Darnold works as a producer for Newschannel 8, a twenty-four-hour local cable news station in Washington, DC. "It's kind of a local CNN," Mike explains. "It was the first of its kind in the country. Now there are several in the larger markets."

Mike's day starts with news gathering before he even arrives at the station: he reads *The Washington Post* and listens to the radio news. With a sense of the day's events, he's able to start his work day with a planning meeting; at this meeting, Mike, another producer, and the assignments editor all decide which news to cover for the thirty-minute newscast.

While the assignments editor takes the responsibility for getting reporters and photographers to events, Mike begins planning the show. He looks at news feeds and the Associated Press news wire, then puts together a tentative outline. "I don't start writing most of my copy until much later, because things tend to change so much: stories die; no one shows up at an

What Is It Like to Be A . . . ?, CONTINUED

event; the story wasn't what we thought it was; something bigger breaks and we have to scrap what we're doing."

Mike is also responsible for making certain that all late-developing details of a report make it on the air, "whether that means telling the reporter on the scene, 'This is what we've learned,' or writing it into the anchor's copy." Mike then coordinates all the players in the newscast so that everyone knows what they're doing during the thirty minutes they're on the air. With so much of a producer's work taking place behind the scenes, Mike emphasizes that a producer has to get used to anonymity among the viewing public. "Everyone knows what an anchor or a reporter does," he says, "but you tell people you're a producer and they haven't a clue what you do."

"Ninety percent of the job is nailing down little loose ends."

Freddy James is another professional toiling away behind the scenes of a cable station. As an associate producer, Freddy works on specials for Home and Garden Television (HGTV), a national cable station based in Knoxville, Tennessee. A recent project focused on Jimmy Carter's Habitat for Humanity program. The program recruits volunteers to build homes for families in need. "We preinterviewed ten families who were to receive homes, and selected three," Freddy says. "We centered the show around them, and around the volunteers who came from all over the world to help them build these homes in one week."

With the other members of the production, Freddy planned the shoot. They set up all hotel and crew arrangements, as well as researched the Habitat for Humanity program. They set up interviews with officials of the program. "And we went to the families' old homes and interviewed them about the project, and how they felt about being a part of it." During the four-day shoot, the production team got footage of the houses going up, and they talked to officials and volunteers. The on-air talent arrived on the scene for a day to shoot his commentary. "We shot thirty thirty-minute tapes of video to wade through," Freddy says.

The producers returned to the network with all this footage, and reviewed the material. "We select our bites," he says, "and start writing the show. Our executive producers proof our scripts, then we set up a voice-over session for our talent, and he voices the script." After selecting video for a program, the producers have it digitized for editing on the computer.

Throughout the Habitat for Humanity shoot, musicians composed music for the show, and graphic artists created designs. Within a month of beginning the project, the piece was submitted to the executives for final approval. Because projects frequently overlap, Freddy began work on another while the Habitat project wrapped up.

HAVE I GOT WHAT IT TAKES TO BE A TELEVISION PRODUCER?

A producer, whether working on series television, newscasts, or specials, must have writing skills—as a producer you'll be writing news copy and scripts. Because you're responsible for bringing together many different elements of a program, you must have good organizational skills. Producers on some projects are responsible for budgeting and other financial concerns, so a head for business can be beneficial to you, as well.

Mike stresses the importance of flexibility to producers. Producers should also be detail-oriented. "Ninety percent of the job," he says, "is nailing down little loose ends." A good disposition is also valuable to producers. "You have to work well with a number of different types of people," Mike says.

Freddy credits his success with his love of the work. "I love being able to tell a story with pictures and words," he says. "I love being able to draw the viewer at home into our story." Working on specials, he also has the advantage of taking on different subjects from project to project. A disadvantage is the stress of putting together a quality program in a short amount of time.

To be a successful TV producer, you should:
- Have well-developed writing skills
- Be organized and detail-oriented
- Have business training so you can deal with budgets and other financial concerns
- Have strong people skills
- Be willing to travel and work long hours
- Be able to handle stress and meet deadlines

HOW DO I BECOME A TELEVISION PRODUCER?

Mike became interested in producing after developing writing skills as a member of a music and drama group. After leaving the group, he pursued a degree in journalism from the University of New Mexico. Mike then landed an unpaid

How Do I Become A . . . ?, continued

internship as a reporter with an ABC affiliate in Albuquerque, followed by a paid internship with an NBC affiliate his senior year of college.

Freddy received a communications degree from the University of Tennessee, Knoxville, where he took courses in speech communication, TV management, and producing. But he got the bulk of his training by working in the field; he got his first job as a studio cameraman for a local news station, while still a junior in college.

Education

High School

It's very important to take composition, English, and other classes that help you to develop writing skills. Journalism courses, with emphasis on news reporting, are valuable. On your high school newspaper or with a school radio station, you may be able to gain some editing and producing experience. A local radio or TV station may offer high school students part-time work or internships.

If you're less interested in news and more interested in entertainment, your drama department could provide you with valuable experience; most theatrical productions require people working behind the scenes to organize, promote, and seek funding. Such experience can give you a sense of a producer's responsibilities.

Postsecondary Training

Producers of news programs are often graduates of journalism schools. Most universities across the country have journalism, or communications, departments, and many of these departments offer courses in broadcasting. Though a broadcast journalism degree is valuable to someone looking for work in TV news, it's not required. Actually, some news departments prefer students with a broader education; many news directors complain that today's journalism school graduates don't have an adequate understanding of history, geography, and political science.

When choosing a journalism school, make sure the school offers opportunities for hands-on experience, whether through participating network affiliates, or through its own broadcasting stations. Also, make sure the school has a good internship program, and that the school makes strong efforts to place its graduating students in jobs.

For those wanting to produce series television, courses offered by a theater or film department can give you a sense of dramatic structure. At a film school, you'll learn much about the business, as well as make connections with people wanting to help young filmmakers.

INTERNSHIPS AND VOLUNTEERSHIPS

An internship with a television news department frequently leads to full-time employment with that same department upon graduation. Because of this, internships can be highly competitive and many students must take nonpaying internships. The paid internships are the most valuable; federal law limits the amount of work unpaid interns are allowed to do for a station. Only with a paid internship can you get the full experience of working for a TV newscast. Your journalism school should have some connections to internships; some schools are visited annually by recruiters from TV and radio stations. Your local stations should also offer internship opportunities. And check the World Wide Web for internship listings from all across the country. Some short-term summer programs are available to journalism students—the Lawrence Wade Journalism Fellowship offers a ten-week salaried internship in Washington, DC, and the Institute on Political Journalism offers a six-week summer program at Georgetown University in Washington, DC.

WHO WILL HIRE ME?

With his first paid internship at an NBC affiliate in Albuquerque, Mike worked full-time at minimum wage, and was frequently on the air. "I talked to the news director about hiring me permanently as a reporter, and he said he wanted me to go to a smaller market for a couple of years to cut my teeth." Mike resisted this idea, and was eventually offered an alternative: a part-time position as producer for a medical segment. The position paid much more than minimum wage, and Mike was actually pleased to have the opportunity to work behind the scenes. "If you're on the air you have to look the look; even off the air you're expected to live in a fish bowl, so to speak."

Mike produced the medical segment for five years, while also working as "special projects producer"—producing series and other projects for the ratings periods. Eventually, he was asked to fill in for a month producing a 5:00 PM newscast. "When management saw my work, they gave me the 6:00 PM show." This then led to his current position with the cable news channel in Washington, DC.

Who Will Hire Me?, continued

Freddy got his first job his junior year of college after a tour of a TV station. "I made sure the executive producer knew who I was when I left that day," he says. While most of the other students were interested in anchoring, Freddy stressed his interest in producing. "And I sent a follow-up letter to the executive producer. The next thing I knew, they called wanting to know if I wanted to run studio camera for minimum wage." The station was number one in the city, so Freddy knew the job would be a good opportunity to get his foot in the door. "I eventually began producing for the station during my last year of college." After only nine months of producing, Freddy was hired by HGTV, based on some special projects he had produced.

Where Can I Go from Here?

Advancement possibilities

- **News anchors** lead the broadcast on-camera; they read news copy from a TelePrompTer and introduce taped and live reports on issues such as health, finance reports, weather, and sports.
- **News directors** lead the news staff, directing the producers, reporters, and editors; determine the newsworthy events to be covered, and assign news staff to specific stories.
- **General managers** manage the operations of TV stations; they're involved in marketing, promotion, contracts, and public relations activities.

Mike hopes to produce documentaries. "I want to get back out into field producing," he says. "I may start my own company or work for a media department within an association." Freddy would like to work in cable management eventually. "I'd love to head the programming department of a network like HGTV," he says, "but I miss live television. I'd love to eventually produce a live show again."

Within a newscast, a producer may move up to news director, or into station management. Some producers for network television move on to produce their own projects for independent production companies.

What Are Some Related Jobs?

The U.S. Department of Labor classifies television producers under the heading, Occupations in Entertainment and Recreation, Not Elsewhere Classified (DOT). Other careers that fall under this classification include stage managers, radio directors, television directors, news anchors, motion-picture directors, radio producers, executive producers, and artist-and-repertoire (A & R) managers. Related careers in the film and radio industries include screenwriters, reporters, art directors, assistant directors, casting directors, assignment editors, directors of photography, film editors, and sound editors.

What Are the Salary Ranges?

Though producers with their own production companies, like producers for network television, can make well over $200,000 a year, most producers working on newscasts make considerably less. Bringing in the big paychecks as a producer for television comes from years of hard work, good luck, and well-established connections. But good producers don't generally enter the field with big money in mind—they love the work. Producers who don't make a great deal of money benefit in other ways: they often call all the shots and have control of a project. They get to make the creative decisions that shape the broadcast.

In smaller markets, a full-time producer of a TV newscast may make as little as $17,000 a year; even in the larger markets, a producer probably won't make more than $40,000. As an executive producer, you can expect a better wage: the median annual salary for an executive producer is around $42,000.

What Is the Job Outlook?

New cable networks with original programming are developing at a rapid rate; and many more networks are expected to develop as technology allows for cable companies to offer more channels. Freelance opportunities will also increase, as these cable companies look to independent production companies for the bulk of their programming. TV producers must keep track of advancing technology—not only will they be required to understand various computer-assisted techniques, but broadcasting is expected to become more closely involved with the Internet and interactive television.

Related Jobs

Art directors
Artist-and-repertoire (A & R) managers
Assignment editors
Assistant directors
Casting directors
Directors of photography
Executive producers
Film editors
Motion-picture directors
News anchors
Production managers
Radio directors
Radio producers
Reporters
Screenwriters
Sound editors
Stage managers
Television directors

What Is the Job Outlook?, continued

Producers will continue to be in demand to put together newscasts: newsrooms provide TV stations with healthy profits every year, and this is not expected to change. The number of news departments and news staff is expected to increase at a steady rate. But the number of students graduating from broadcast journalism departments is also growing. There are currently over two hundred broadcast journalism programs in the country, and their students don't account for all the people seeking work in broadcasting; because news directors hire graduates from many different programs (and some *prefer* to hire graduates with more well-rounded liberal arts degrees), there's growing competition for the available positions.

Weather Forecaster

SUMMARY

DEFINITION
Weather forecasters *compile and analyze weather information, and prepare reports for daily and nightly newscasts. They create graphics, write scripts, and explain weather maps to audiences. They also provide special reports during extreme weather conditions.*

ALTERNATIVE JOB TITLES
Broadcast meteorologist
Weathercaster
Weather reporter

SALARY RANGE
$25,000 to $40,000 to $300,000+

EDUCATIONAL REQUIREMENTS
Bachelor's degree

CERTIFICATION OR LICENSING
Voluntary

EMPLOYMENT OUTLOOK
Little change or more slowly than the average

HIGH SCHOOL SUBJECTS
Agriculture
Chemistry
Earth science
Mathematics
Speech

PERSONAL INTERESTS
Broadcasting
Computers
Current Events
The Environment
Helping people: protection
Science

Still stuck at the TV station after two full days, Ed Piotrowski wades through the constantly changing weather information transmitted from the Hurricane Center, the Severe Storms Forecast Center, and other sources. The hurricane has approached Myrtle Beach, South Carolina, and people are keeping close to their radios and TVs. They're all relying on Ed, and the other meteorologists in the region, to provide them with reliable information—they're listening closely to all broadcast reports to help them determine what precautions to take to protect their homes and their lives.

Interrupting regular programming, Ed broadcasts live from in front of his computer equipment. He very calmly relates the information he has analyzed, telling his viewers everything he can about the hurricane—its position, where it's expected to go, and what it will mean to the city. Though these storms are unpredictable and frightening, Ed takes it as his responsibility to inform and instruct his viewers, to keep them calm and safe.

What Does a Weather Forecaster Do?

El Niño. F5-rated tornadoes storming down tornado alley. Heat waves and ice storms. Flood-started fires in North Dakota. Hurricanes Andrew, Hugo, and Betsy. Extreme weather conditions often become national celebrities while the citizens of the threatened cities suffer. These people look to TV and radio weather forecasters to advise them of upcoming storms, how to prepare for them, and how to recover from them. But weather forecasters aren't just on the air during extreme conditions—they're on radio and TV broadcasts many times every day. Though one day you may be relying on your local forecaster to help you prepare for a midnight tornado, another day you may simply want to know whether to leave the house with an umbrella.

Some weather forecasters are reporters with broadcasting degrees, but over half of TV and radio weather forecasters have degrees in meteorology. Meteorology is the science of the atmosphere, and colleges across the country offer courses and degrees in meteorology for people who want to work for broadcast stations, weather services, research centers, flight centers, universities, and other places that study and record the weather. With a good background in the atmospheric sciences, broadcast weather forecasters can make informed predictions about the weather, and can clearly explain these predictions to the public.

Lingo to Learn

Advisory: *A report on weather conditions that may lead to hazards but don't pose immediate dangers.*

Barometer: *An instrument that measures atmospheric pressure.*

Cold front: *The edge of a cold air mass that moves forward and displaces warmer air, leading to dropping temperatures and humidity.*

Doppler radar: *An electronic instrument that measures atmospheric motion of objects such as precipitation.*

Heat index: *Not the actual temperature, but a number that describes the combination of temperature and humidity.*

NEXRAD: *Next-generation weather radar; a network of Doppler radars.*

The weather centers of your local radio and TV stations compile data from a variety of sources. They interpret the data, and report it to the viewing and listening public. The data they receive is compiled by various weather stations around the world—even the weather conditions swirling over the oceans can affect the weather of states far inland, so your local weather forecaster keeps track of the weather affecting distant cities. Weather stations and ships at sea record atmospheric measurements, information that is then transmitted to other weather stations for analysis. This information makes its way to the National Weather Service in Washington, DC, where meteorologists develop forecasts, then send them on to regional centers across the country. Broadcast weather forecasters receive this data. They also

Wild storm facts:

*After a tornado stormed through Great Bend, Kansas, five horses, unhurt and still hitched to the same rail, were found a quarter mile from their demolished barn.

*The Chicago Blizzard of 1967 dropped 23 inches of snow in less than a half hour; the 23 million tons of snow stopped the city in its tracks, stranding cars, buses, and trains.

*Agnes, Beulah, Hazel, Inez—not the names of women in a sewing circle, but the names of hurricanes that have been "retired" because of the amount of damage they've caused. Hurricane Agnes of 1972 produced floods that contributed to 122 deaths and 6.4 billion dollars in damage.

read information from radar, computers, satellites, and charts.

With the aid of computers, broadcast weather forecasters turn all this data into your daily weather report. They prepare maps and graphics to aid the viewers. Broadcasting the information means reading and explaining the weather forecast to viewers and listeners. Many people look to TV and radio news for weather information to help them plan events and vacations. Farmers are often able to protect their crops by following weather forecasts and advisories. The weather forecast is a staple element of most TV and radio newscasts. Some cable and radio stations broadcast weather reports twenty-four-hours a day; most local network affiliates broadcast reports during morning, noon, and evening newscasts, as well as provide extended weather coverage during storms and other extreme conditions.

In addition to broadcasting weather reports, radio and TV weather forecasters often visit schools and community centers to speak on weather safety. They are also frequently involved in broadcast station promotions, taking part in community events.

What Is It Like to Be a Weather Forecaster?

The people of Myrtle Beach, South Carolina, look to Ed Piotrowski of WPDE-TV for information on approaching hurricanes and other weather events. "Don't go into TV weather just to be on TV," Ed advises. "You must have a passion for the weather to do a fantastic job." Ed has had this passion ever since he was a kid. "All through grade school I would run out and tell people all about the weather." This passion eventually led him to an internship that helped him realize that TV was the place for him. "I realized how cool it is to be the first person to tell everyone about weather changes." As chief meteorologist for WPDE, Ed is responsible for delivering the forecast for radio and four television evening newscasts. "I also manage a staff of three, and several interns."

His day often begins with a visit to a local school, where he talks to students about weather and safety. The visit is tape recorded for later broadcast. "I

What Is It Like to Be a . . . ?, continued

head to the weather center at around 2:00 PM and prepare graphics and the forecast for the nightly shows." After shows at 5:00 PM and 6:00 PM, Ed takes a dinner break then returns for the 10:00 PM and 11:00 PM shows.

Preparing the forecast means interpreting a great deal of data from a variety of different sources. The station receives weather information from the National Center for Environmental Prediction, the Storm Prediction Center (formerly known as the National Hurricane Center), the local National Weather Service offices, and the Severe Storms Forecast Center. Data also comes in from many different cities around the world. "All the data collected is put into many computer programs with various scientific formulas. These programs eventually put out weather scenarios for several different times in the future. Our job is to interpret these and make our forecast accordingly."

Though Ed relies on his education and background in meteorology to work with the various tools of the weather center, he points out that weather computers vary in their operation. "Most of this is learned on the job," he says. And the technology is rapidly changing. "Doppler radar is relatively new. The computers are getting fancier and faster."

> **"Don't go into TV weather just to be on TV. You must have a passion for the weather to do a fantastic job."**

While presenting the forecast on the air, Ed is doing many things behind the scenes. "There's a lot of switching and moving around that the viewer doesn't see because we are masking it with graphics." The viewing audience sees Ed in front of a weather map, but actually he's just standing in front of a plain blue wall called a "chromakey." Ed watches the monitor for the visuals, and points to the map based on what he sees on the TV screen. During the forecast, the newscast producer gives Ed time cues (the amount of time left in the presentation) through an IFB—a hearing device hidden in Ed's ear.

During hurricanes, Ed has even more responsibilities—and a whole different set of rules. "People like to see someone they think is their friend. But during hurricanes, we don't want to be on TV joking around. We need to interpret the data to give people the scenario we think will play out in our area upon landfall. It could be the difference between life and death."

Have I Got What It Takes to Be a Weather Forecaster?

To be a good weather forecaster, you need to have a strong interest in weather and the environment. An understanding of math and science is important to a broadcast meteorologist because using charts and formulas is essential to predicting the weather. You should also have computer skills, as you'll be using computer data transmitted from weather centers, as well as preparing graphics for broadcast. Because you'll be on air a lot, you should have good speaking skills and be capable of clearly explaining weather maps and forecasts.

To be a successful weather forecaster, you should:

Have a strong interest in the weather and the environment in general

Be good at math and science and have computer skills

Speak clearly and be able to explain weather maps, conditions, forecasts, and other meteorological data

Have an outgoing personality and enjoy meeting people and participating in community-related events

"To be successful," Ed says, "it's important to have an outgoing personality as well as a solid background in meteorology. You need the personality on light weather days, and you really need good meteorology skills when talking about hurricanes." Ed appreciates the opportunities to meet a lot of people and to attend many events. And he appreciates his viewers' patience with the uncertainty of weather forecasts. "You can blow the forecast and still have a job the next day!"

But Ed wishes he could have a more regular schedule; his schedule depends on the radar. "And it can be demanding with all the public appearances you make," he says.

How Do I Become a Weather Forecaster?

Ed received a BS in Meteorology from North Carolina State, then learned a great deal about TV weather from an internship with WCTI-TV in North Carolina. "It was the best thing I ever did to start my career," he says. "It taught me many things that I didn't learn in college. It was great on-the-job experience." Ed got this training on his own, by actually calling the TV station and asking if he could come in and watch the weather department at work. "Next thing you know, I was spending three

Fast Fact

Would you believe that late night funnyman David Letterman was once a TV weather forecaster in his native Indiana? During his short career he once predicted hail the size of canned hams!

to five days a week there learning all about TV weather. It was tough to understand at first, but the more I did things, the more I learned about being an on-camera meteorologist."

Education

High School
Math and science courses will help you prepare for a college meteorology program. Join a school science group, or organize one that focuses on atmospheric research. You should also take English and composition courses to develop your writing skills. If you don't have any experience with computer graphics programs, take a computer class. Become involved with your high school newspaper or radio station to gain broadcast experience. Visit the weather departments of your local radio and TV stations, or any other local weather service centers.

Postsecondary Training
Though a degree in meteorology isn't required of broadcast weather forecasters, it is very valuable—and you'll need such a degree to advance in the profession. Talk to your high school guidance counselor about these programs. The American Meteorological Society (AMS) publishes a listing of schools, with extensive information about each program. Check your school or local library for a copy, or purchase one from the AMS.

Over one hundred programs are listed in the AMS publication; these programs offer such courses as atmospheric measurements, thermodynamics and chemistry, radar, cloud dynamics, and physical climatology.

Certification or Licensing

There is no certification in broadcast meteorology, but the AMS and the National Weather Association (NWA) do each offer a "seal of approval." To qualify for the AMS seal, applicants must have completed twelve semester hours of college study in specific areas of meteorology. They must also submit taped samples of their work for review by an evaluation board. For the NWA seal, broadcast meteorologists must meet these same requirements, and must also pass a multiple-choice exam.

An AMS or NWA seal of approval isn't required for broadcast weather forecasters to work in the business, but it will give you an edge when looking for a job. Some stations list the seal of approval in their job advertisements. The

AMS is also looking into requiring continuing education courses for seal renewal.

INTERNSHIPS AND VOLUNTEERSHIPS

Most local radio and TV stations have internship opportunities for student weather forecasters. If your school doesn't have an internship program, contact the chief meteorologists of local stations. Internships offer valuable experience, and often lead to full-time employment. There can be a lot of competition for paid internships, however, and you may have to make do with volunteer work for a station to gain experience. Though your duties are limited in a volunteer situation, you can still learn a lot about the business and make connections. Some undergraduate programs offer students paid research opportunities, but most research and teaching assistantships are open only to graduate students.

WHO WILL HIRE ME?

Ed's first full-time job was with the TV station where he interned. "I was very fortunate," he says. "I showed great initiative and the weekend job opened up right around the time I graduated." Ed held the weekend position for one year, then went to work on the station's morning newscast for two years. He's held his current position as chief meteorologist at WPDE-TV for four years.

If your internship doesn't lead to full-time job opportunities, you can check your local ads or job listings on the Internet. The AMS and NWA send members job listings, and also post job openings on their Web pages. Most broadcast meteorologists work for network television affiliates and local radio stations; because evening national newscasts don't have weather forecasts, there are few network opportunities for broadcast meteorologists. National cable networks like The Weather Channel and twenty-four-hour news channels hire weather forecasters and offer internships.

With a degree in meteorology, you can work for a variety of other services as well—the United States government is the largest

Advancement possibilities

Chief meteorologists head the weather centers of newscasts; they direct staffs of weather reporters, assistants, and interns.

News anchors host radio and television newscasts.

General managers manage the daily operations of TV and radio stations; they're involved in marketing, promotion, contracts, and public relations.

Who Will Hire Me?, continued

employer of meteorologists in the country. Meteorologists work for the National Weather Service, the military, the Department of Agriculture, and other agencies.

Where Can I Go from Here?

"Many weather people strive to get to the big cities to make the big money," Ed says. "I used to think that way; but I now believe that finding a good place that pays nicely is what matters the most. Getting to the big markets can be hard, and difficult to stay in." Ed will also continue to develop his meteorology skills by taking courses. "The field changes so much, you would be an idiot not to attend some of the various seminars and conferences that are offered throughout the year." Ed regularly attends the Hurricane Conference, the AMS conference, and one other, such as a Doppler Radar or satellite conference.

Someone forecasting for a network affiliate in a smaller region may want to move to a larger city and a larger audience. In many cases, though, meteorologists work up within one station. Full-time broadcast meteorologists generally start forecasting for the weekend news, or the morning news, then move up to the evening news. A meteorologist may then become chief meteorologist, in charge of a newscast's weather center and staff.

What Are Some Related Jobs?

The U.S. Department of Labor classifies weather forecasters under the heading, Occupations in Meteorology (DOT). Occupations classified under this heading include *hydrographers,* who determine trends in the movement and utilization of water; *oceanographic assistants,* who record and study oceanographic and meteorological data to predict changes in weather and sea conditions; and *weather observers,* who collect and record data on weather conditions for use in forecasting.

The U.S. Department of Labor also classifies weather forecasters under the heading, Laboratory Technology: Physical Sciences (GOE for meteorological technicians). Some related jobs include stratigraphers, mathematicians, seismologists, geologists, geophysicists, physicists, mineralogists, and climatologists.

Additionally, the work of weather forecasters is comparable to other on-air broadcasting careers such as reporters, sportscasters, news anchors, and disc jockeys.

What Are the Salary Ranges?

In the newsroom, weather forecasters generally make more than sportscasters but less than lead anchors. The salary for weather forecasters varies greatly according to experience and region. In some of the smallest markets, a weather forecaster can expect to make around $25,000 per year; in the largest markets, a weather forecaster may make $100,000. The median for forecasters across the country is around $40,000.

In some top stations in large cities, a TV weather forecaster can become something of a local celebrity, attracting higher ratings for the station. Popular weather forecasters with large audiences have been known to command over $300,000 a year.

Related Jobs
Climatologists
Disc jockeys
Geologists
Geophysicists
Hydrographers
Mathematicians
Mineralogists
News anchors
Oceanographic assistants
Physicists
Reporters
Seismologists
Sportscasters
Stratigraphers
Weather observers

What Is the Job Outlook?

Meteorology is greatly affected by technological advances. New tools and computer programs for the compilation and analyses of data are constantly being developed by research scientists. Future broadcast meteorologists will need a lot of technical expertise, in addition to their understanding of weather. With these projected developments, forecasters will be able to predict the weather weeks in advance, and someday, even months in advance.

Usually, meteorologists are able to find work in the field upon graduation, though they may have to be flexible about the area of meteorology and region of the country in which they work. Positions for broadcast meteorologists, as with any positions in broadcast news, are in high demand. The number of news departments and news staff is expected to increase at a steady rate, but the growing number of graduates looking for work in news departments will keep the field very competitive. Currently about half of TV and radio

What Is the Job Outlook?, continued

weather forecasters do not hold meteorology degrees; with increased competition for work, forecasters without extensive backgrounds in the atmospheric sciences may find it difficult to get jobs.

But a national fascination with weather may lead to more outlets for broadcast meteorologists. Look for more cable weather information channels like the Weather Channel to develop. Weather disasters are requiring more coverage by news departments; in addition to forecasting, broadcast meteorologists will be involved in reporting about the aftereffects of storms and other extreme conditions. Many people look to the Internet for global and regional weather information, so look for broadcast and Internet weather resources to merge. Broadcast meteorologists are becoming more actively involved in developing and maintaining pages on the World Wide Web.

Section 3

What Can I Do Right Now?

radio & tv

Get Involved: A Directory of Camps, Programs, Internships, Etc.

First

Now that you've read about some of the different careers available in radio and television broadcasting, you may be anxious to experience this line of work for yourself, to find out what it's *really* like. Or perhaps you already feel certain that this is the career path for you and want to get started on it right away. Whichever is the case, this section is for you! There are plenty of things you can do right now to learn about broadcasting careers while gaining valuable experience. Just as important, you'll get to meet new friends and see new places, too.

In the following pages you will find more than twenty programs run by organizations that want to work with young people interested in radio and television. All of them can help you turn your interest into a career, but none of them will prevent you from changing your mind or just keeping your options open. Some organizations offer just one kind of program: colleges, quite naturally, will probably offer only academic courses of study. Other organizations, such as TV stations, may offer internships and job opportunities in addition to voluntary field experiences. It's up to you to decide whether you're interested in one particular type of program or are open to a number of possibilities. The kinds of activities available are listed right after the name of the program or organization, so you can skim through to find the listings that interest you most.

The Categories

Camps
When you see an activity that is classified as a camp, don't automatically start packing your tent and mosquito repellent. Particularly where academic study is involved, the term "camp" sometimes simply means a residential program including both educational and recreational activities. However, some broadcasting programs do take place in conventional camps. That means that many of the camps in this volume do include actual camping, including outdoor activities and living in log cabins—although you're not likely to need the tent. Since there are a number of camps of both kinds listed here, be sure to read the descriptions thoroughly so you can tell the difference.

College Courses/Summer Study
These terms are linked because most college courses offered to students your age must take place in the summer, when you are out of school. On the other hand, many summer study programs are sponsored by colleges and universities that want to attract future students and give them a head start in higher education. Summer study of almost any type is a good idea because it keeps your mind and your study skills sharp over the long vacation. Summer study at a college offers any number of additional benefits, including giving you the tools to make a well-informed decision about your future academic career. We have included many study options in these listings, including some outstanding college and university broadcasting programs.

Employment Opportunities
As you may already know from experience, employment opportunities for teenagers can be very limited. This is particularly true in competitive fields such as radio and television broadcasting. There *are* a few jobs in the field for high school students, but you may just have to earn your money by working at a mall or restaurant and get your broadcasting experience in an unpaid position somewhere else. Bear in mind that, if you do a good enough job and the station or organization you work for has the funding, this summer's volunteer or shadow position could be next summer's job.

Field Experience

This is something of a catchall category for activities that don't exactly fit the other descriptions. There are a few listings in this volume that are classified as both field experiences and volunteer opportunities. More often than not, such listings are your chance to shadow a broadcasting professional. If you shadow more than once or twice, you may have the chance to do some volunteer work for your pro. Because they are so flexible, such field experiences are perfect for students who want to explore radio and television a bit more before making any kind of career decision.

Internships

Basically, an internship combines the responsibilities of a job (strict schedules, pressing duties, and usually written evaluations by your supervisor) with the uncertainties of a volunteer position (no wages or fringe benefits, no guarantee of future employment). That may not sound very enticing, but completing an internship is a great way to prove your maturity, your commitment to broadcasting, and your knowledge and skills to colleges, potential employers, and yourself. Some internships are just formalized volunteer positions, others offer unique responsibilities and opportunities: choose the kind that works best for you!

Memberships

When an organization is in this category, it simply means that you are welcome to pay your dues and become a card-carrying member. Formally joining any organization has the benefits of meeting others who share your interests and concerns, finding opportunities to take action, and keeping up with current events in the field and in the group. Depending on how active you are, the contacts you make and experiences you gain may help when the time comes to apply to colleges or look for a job.

In some organizations, you may pay a special student rate but receive virtually the same benefits as a regular adult member. Other groups have student branches with special activities and publications. Don't let membership dues discourage you from contacting any of these organizations. Most charge low fees because they know that students are perpetually short of funds. If the fees are still too much for you, contact the group that interests you anyway—they are likely to at least send you some information and place you on their mailing list.

Volunteer Opportunities

Many of the volunteer opportunities listed here allow you to shadow a broadcasting professional and, depending on how that experience goes, eventually volunteer to help that professional around the radio or TV station. You can also find volunteer opportunities at most public television and radio stations around the United States, particularly in their fundraising departments. Depending on your needs and interests, volunteering can be a long- or short-term commitment, perhaps part-time during the school year or full-time during a pledge drive. This is an option that is flexible and broad enough for almost everyone.

Program Descriptions

Once you've started to look at the individual listings themselves, you'll find that they contain a lot of information. Naturally, there is a general description of the program(s), but wherever possible we also have included the following details.

Application Information

Each listing notes how far in advance you'll need to apply for the program or position, but the simple rule is to apply as far in advance as possible. This ensures that you won't miss out on a great opportunity simply because other people got there ahead of you. It also means that you will get a timely decision on your application, so if you are not accepted, you'll still have some time to apply elsewhere. As for the things that make up your application—essays, recommendations, etc.—we've tried to tell you what's involved, but be sure to contact the program about specific requirements before you submit anything.

Background Information

This includes such information as the date the program was established, the name of the organization that is sponsoring it financially, and the faculty and staff who will be there for you. This can help you—and your family—gauge the quality and reliability of the program.

Classes and Activities

Classes and activities change from year to year, but knowing that a precollege program usually offers "Introduction to Radio Broadcasting" or that a camp generally includes a field trip to a local television station can help you decide if it's the right kind of program for you.

Contact Information

Wherever possible, we have given the *title* of the person whom you should contact instead of the *name* because people change jobs so frequently. If no title is given and you are telephoning an organization, simply tell the person who answers the phone the name of the program or position that interests you and he or she will forward your call. If you are writing, include the line "Attention: Summer Study Program" (or whatever is appropriate after "Attention") somewhere on the envelope. This will help to ensure that your letter goes to the person in charge of that program.

Credit

Where academic programs (and a few internships) are concerned, we sometimes note that high school or college credit is available to those who have completed them. This means that the program can count toward your high school diploma or a future college degree just like a regular course. Obviously, this can be very useful, but it's important to note that rules about accepting such credit vary from school to school and college to college. Before you commit to a program offering high school credit, check with your guidance counselor to see if it is accepted at your school. As for programs offering college credit, check with your chosen college (if you have one) to see if they will accept it.

Eligibility and Qualifications

The main eligibility requirement to be concerned about is age or grade in school. A term frequently used in relation to grade level is "rising," as in "rising senior," someone who will be a senior when the next school year begins. This is especially important where summer programs are concerned. Some organizations base admissions decisions partly on GPA, class rank, and standardized test scores. This is mentioned in the listings, but you must contact the program for specific numbers. If you are worried that your GPA or your ACT scores, for example, aren't good enough, don't let them stop you from applying to programs that consider such things in the admissions process. Often, a fine essay or even an example of your dedication and eagerness can compensate for statistical weaknesses.

Facilities

Of course you need to know if you'll be roughing it out in the woods or relaxing in a new dormitory on a college campus. But you should also know about the production facilities and equipment you'll be using. Modern equipment and cutting-edge technology tend to play a large part in this career field, so you'll want to inquire as to the nature of the facilities if it's not covered here.

Financial Details
You'll definitely want to know if you'll be paying or getting paid, and just how much money is involved! Prices do tend to go up each year, but they should be close to the figures we quote. We always try to note where financial aid is available, but most programs will do their best to ensure a shortage of funds does not stop you from taking part.

Residential vs. Commuter Options
Simply put, some programs prefer that participating students live with other participants and staff members, others do not, and still others leave the decision entirely to the students themselves. As a rule, residential programs are suitable for young people who live out of town or even out of state, as well as for local residents. Commuter programs may be viable only if you live near the program site or if you can stay with relatives who do. Bear in mind that for residential programs especially, the travel between your home and the location of the activity is almost always your responsibility and can significantly increase the cost of participation. Some programs make special provision for transporting you to the program site from the nearest airport or major city.

FINALLY . . .

Ultimately, there are three important things to bear in mind concerning all of the programs listed in this volume. The first is that things change. Staff members come and go, funding is added and withdrawn, supply and demand determine which programs continue and which terminate. Dates, times, and costs vary widely because of a number of factors. Because of this, the information we give you, although as current and detailed as possible, is just not enough on which to base your final decision. If you are interested in a program, you simply must write, call, fax, or email the organization in charge to get the latest and most complete information available. This has the added benefit of putting you in touch with someone who can help you with your individual questions and problems.

Another important consideration is that the editors of this volume do not actually endorse any of the programs or organizations listed here. We have not attended the programs or seen their facilities; instead, we are just passing the information they gave us on to you. You must do some research of your own and make your own decisions as to what is right for you.

The third thing to bear in mind is that the programs listed here are just the tip of the iceberg. No book can possibly cover all of the opportunities that are available to you—partly because they are so numerous and are constantly coming and going, but partly because some are waiting to be discovered. For instance, you may be very interested in an internship at a television station several hundred miles away from you. Instead of complaining about the distance, why not go to one of your local stations and ask if you could arrange an internship there? They may already have a program for you to join or they may start one because you were the first person to show an interest. Or perhaps you would like to take a college course but don't see the college that interests you in the listings. Call their Admissions Office! Even if they don't have a special program for high school students, they might be able to arrange for you to visit or sit in on a class. Use the ideas behind these listings and take the initiative to turn them into opportunities!

THE PROGRAMS

ADVANCED TELEVISION TEST CENTER

Internship

The Advanced Television Test Center (ATTC) explores the future of TV viewing, and right now the future is in high-definition television. Already available in Europe and Japan, high-definition television features enhanced color and the ability to perceive depth on the TV screen. If you have a keen interest in electronics and learning how to operate television equipment, the center offers paid internships to high school students at a minimum rate of $5 per hour. If you're a highly motivated, independent student with some knowledge of electronic theory, this might be the place to prepare a career for yourself in the futuristic world of what is essentially 3-D television. Interns typically do some production and editing, work with the audio and video engineers on different projects, and spend time with the tape librarian. The ATTC is willing to work with any school and any student who is serious about a career in electronics engineering. Most students intern in the summer, but other seasons can be considered. Work-study is also an option. No housing is available, though, so you must either live in the area or be able to stay with someone who does. Your initial approach to the Advanced Television Test Center should be a resume and a letter that states your interest and background. You can also call or write for more details.

■ **Advanced Television Test Center**
1330 Braddock Place, Suite 200
Alexandria, VA 22314
Tel: 703-739-3850

AMERICAN COLLEGIATE ADVENTURES
College Course/Summer Study

American Collegiate Adventures (ACA) offers high school students the chance to experience and prepare for college during summer vacation. Adventures are based at Arizona State University in Tempe and the University of Wisconsin in Madison; they vary in length from three to six weeks. Participants attend college-level courses taught by university faculty during the week (for college credit or enrichment) and visit regional colleges and recreation sites over the weekend. All students live in comfortable en suite accommodations, just down the hall from an ACA resident staff member. Courses differ from year to year and place to place, but students interested in broadcasting can usually take "TV Production" and other classes involving both communications and technology. Contact American Collegiate Adventures for the current course listings, prices, and application procedures.

■ **American Collegiate Adventures**
666 North Dundee Road, Suite 803
Northbrook, IL 60062
Tel: 800-509-SUMR or 847-509-9900
Email: ACASUMR@aol.com

BUCK'S ROCK CAMP
Camp

Buck's Rock Camp, about eighty-five miles from New York, has been in existence since 1942. It features forty different activities in creative, performing, and visual arts. The camp has its very own radio station, WBBC 88.5 FM. Here, as a radio broadcaster, you put on your own radio shows and act as a DJ for your favorite music. WBBC broadcasts news, reviews, talk shows, radio plays, and documentaries as well as music. You can work as an announcer, script writer, or commentator. Experienced disc jockeys help you plan the content of your productions and understand the techniques of radio broadcasting.

Buck's Rock Camp is for twelve- to sixteen-year-olds who are artistic, talented, and independent. At camp, you make your own schedule and participate in as many activities as you want to. You may spend all of your time at WBBC, or you may combine your broadcasting with the artistic and sports programs also on offer. Many students return to Buck's Rock year after year and go on to become counselors. If you're sixteen to eighteen years old, you can register for the Counselors in Training program and spend part of your day as a camper and part as a counselor. In this program, you receive a reduction in camp tuition.

Buck's Rock Camp has one four-week and one eight-week session. Tuition for four weeks costs $3,350; the full season costs $5,590. This includes everything but transportation to the camp. Campers stay in cabins, eat in the dining room, and enjoy a full schedule of evening activities. You can get financial aid to help with tuition, and Buck's Rock likes to help as many campers as possible. To apply to the camp, you must fill out an enrollment form and attend a personal interview. To get your form, and to learn more, call, write, or email the camp. You can also visit its Web site.

Buck's Rock Camp
59 Buck's Rock Road
New Milford, CT 06776
Tel: 800-636-5218
Web: http://bucksrock.olm.net
Email: buckrock@ix.netcom.com

Camp Chi

Camp

Camp Chi, located near the beautiful Wisconsin Dells, features many activities in the fine arts, athletics, and outdoor adventure. Included in the arts category are radio and TV broadcasting. This camp features "specialty programs," in which you get to choose three different areas to thoroughly explore during the four-week camp session. If you choose radio, for example, you spend one-third of your time at the camp's WCHI radio station, learning all about radio broadcasting: how to operate the systems, interview talk-show guests, produce and direct shows, and be a DJ for your favorite music. After radio, you may move on to your second specialty area, such as TV. Camp Chi has its own video studio where you can produce and direct TV shows, shoot and edit footage, and write scripts. TV and radio production is supervised by a staff member in that particular field. Your third specialty area could be a sport, such as rollerblading or water polo, an outdoor adventure like rock climbing or outdoor cooking, or another one of the arts. Campers can also study the environment and pioneering. At Camp Chi, there are over thirty areas to choose from.

In addition to all the activities, the camp has a heated swimming pool, a spring-fed lake with waterfront activities, a climbing and rappelling wall, a roller hockey arena, rope courses, six tennis courts, and an animal farm. The staff-to-camper ratio is one to five, and each session usually has four to five hundred campers. Camp Chi is for students ages nine to sixteen. You stay in cabins with built-in bunk beds, twelve campers to a cabin. If you're fourteen to sixteen years old, Camp Chi offers a separate village just for teens. The cost of the camp is $2,150 and that includes everything but transportation to the site. Scholarships are available, based on need. For an enrollment form, and to learn more about the camp, you can write, call, or email. Visit Camp Chi's Web site, too.

■ Camp Chi
<u>Summer Office:</u> PO Box 104
Lake Delton, WI 53940
Tel: 608-253-1681
Web: http://www.campchi.com
Email: campchi@mcimail.com
<u>Winter Office:</u> 3050 Woodridge Road
Northbrook, IL 60062-7599
Tel: 847-272-2301

MANITOU-WABING SPORTS AND ARTS CENTER
Camp

Manitou-Wabing Sports and Arts Center, located in the woods on Manitou-Wabing Lake, offers camping sessions ranging from one to seven weeks. One of its best features is a unique radio broadcasting program that introduces you to all aspects of radio life: planning programs, announcing, writing, reporting, interviewing guests, operating the equipment, newscasting, being a disc jockey of your favorite music, and producing radio drama and quiz shows. If you choose to work at the radio station, you broadcast to the whole camp. One-week sessions, however, do not offer radio broadcasting.

Manitou-Wabing campers usually major in one specific course (radio broadcasting for you!) and minor in several others. If you're really ambitious, you can pick two majors. You spend three to four hours a day in your major and about two hours a day in your minors. You can minor in the arts—ballet, tap, point, and jazz dance; theater; black-and-white photography; drawing and painting; sculpture—or in sports—tennis, waterskiing, golf, horseback riding, swimming, and sailing, to name a few. At night, there's scheduled evening events to enhance your experience. Manitou-Wabing has about 450 campers in every session. The base fee to attend camp, in Canadian dollars, ranges from $4,095 for seven weeks to $1,495 for two weeks. No scholarships are available. The price includes everything you need except transportation to the camp. To register, call, write, email, or visit the camp's Web site.

■**Camp Manitou-Wabing Sports and Arts Center**
Summer Office: McKeller, Ontario, Canada P0G 1C0
Tel: 705-389-2410
Web: http://www.manitou-online.com
Email: camp@manitou-online.com
Winter Office: 77 Ingram Drive, Suite 200
Toronto, Ontario, Canada M6M 2L7
Tel: 416-245-0605

CORNELL UNIVERSITY SUMMER COLLEGE
College Course/Summer Study

Cornell University's Summer College is a program that allows students completing their junior or senior year to explore potential career paths while earning college credit and experiencing campus life. Students live on campus for six weeks in July and August, taking two courses for credit and one noncredit Exploration Seminar for insight into a specific career. The Exploration Seminar in Communication is perfect for those considering a career in broadcasting, or in the related fields of journalism, publishing, and public relations. When the seminar meets, twice each week, participants meet communications professionals, visit newspaper offices and radio and TV stations, and learn how to produce a show on public access television, among other things. To complement this seminar, students choose at least one course in communications: "History of Television" and "Contemporary Mass Communication" are excellent options. You may choose your second course from any of the classes on offer. The courses are taught at a college level, so be prepared for challenging material and a heavy workload. A little time management, however, will give you enough free time to take advantage of the university's many cultural, sporting, and recreational events. Tuition, room and board, and the cost of group activities result in a program fee of about $5,000. Books, supplies, and travel to and from Cornell are additional expenses. Some financial aid is available to deserving students who might not otherwise be able to attend. Contact the Summer College for an application and further details about the courses and seminars on offer.

■**Cornell University Summer College**
B20 Day Hall
Ithaca, NY 14852-2801
Tel: 607-255-6203
Web: http://www.sce.cornell.edu/html/sc.html
Email: sc@sce.cornell.edu

Corporation for Public Broadcasting
Employment Opportunity, Internship, Volunteer Program

The Corporation for Public Broadcasting (CPB) is a private, nonprofit organization that oversees American public radio, television, and on-line services. It is constantly updating its employment and internship opportunities. Most of its job openings are for adults with at least some college, but you still might want to access the CPB Jobline on the Internet or by telephone. You can also write to the CPB for the latest edition of its *Guide to Volunteer and Internship Programs*. This generally has far more listings applicable to high school students.

- **Corporation for Public Broadcasting**
  901 E Street, NW
  Washington, DC 20004-2037
  Jobline: 202-393-1045
  Web: http://www.cpb.org

Eagle Communications (KECI-TV, KCFW-TV, KTVM-TV)
Employment Opportunity

Eagle Communications, which runs NBC channels KECI-TV, KCFW-TV, and KTVM-TV, often has part-time positions for high school students interested in the technical aspects of broadcasting. In the past, students have been hired to help out during newscasts by performing tasks such as camera work and technical direction. Students have also worked as tape and graphics operators. For more information on the current positions available, contact Eagle Communications.

- **Eagle Communications (KECI-TV, KCFW-TV, KTVM-TV)**
  PO Box 5268
  Missoula, MT 59806
  Tel: 406-721-2063

High School Summer Institute
College Course/Summer Study

Columbia College Chicago invites students with an interest in radio or television broadcasting to attend its High School Summer Institute, which runs from mid-July to mid-August. Applicants must have completed their sophomore, junior, or senior year of high school. Participants may choose to commute or live on campus. The residential option means living in the heart of downtown Chicago, but all students can participate in walking tours and excursions to area museums and concerts. When applying, you select between one and three courses in the area or areas that interest you. In recent years, Columbia has offered around four courses in television and as many as six in radio; some are for beginning students, others are for those in their second year at the High School Summer Institute. Previous course topics have included "Creating a Television Program," "Introduction to Radio Production," and "Audio as a Profession." All courses are taught by the regular Columbia College Chicago faculty and most include field trips and hands-on experiences. Students who successfully complete their course(s) receive college credit from Columbia.

Admissions are on a first come, first served basis: it is up to each student to decide whether or not he or she is ready for college-level coursework. Tuition fees range from about $200 to $300 per course, depending on the number of credit hours it is worth. Students selecting the residential option must pay an additional $200 per week for their room; an optional meal plan is extra. Applications for the limited number of scholarships that are available must be received by early May, which is about one month before the general admissions deadline. These courses fill up fast. Contact Columbia College Chicago for more information, including an application form and the latest course offerings.

■ **High School Summer Institute**
Columbia College Chicago
600 South Michigan Avenue
Chicago, IL 60605
Tel: 312-663-1600

THE INTERNATIONAL RADIO AND TELEVISION SOCIETY
Membership

This society is dedicated to keeping its members informed about the increasingly complex world of electronic media. Its student programs are primarily geared toward those at the college level, but high school students can join now to gain insight into the field of broadcasting. Be advised that most of the society's activities, such as its summer fellowship program and minority career workshop—take place in the New York area. As a student, you can join the International Radio and Television Society for about $30, a small price to pay to join fellow members such as Phil Donahue, Peter Arnett, and Diane Sawyer. Write, call, or fax the society for more information on the benefits of membership.

■ **The International Radio and Television Society**
420 Lexington Avenue, Suite 1714
New York, NY 10170-0101
Tel: 212-867-6650

KAID-TV

Internship

KAID-TV, a public television station, offers internships and occasional contract work to high school students. Duties and hours are determined by the student's interests and the station's needs. However, interns frequently work on such tasks as Web page design. Paid positions that are often available include that of runner (usually requiring about ten hours per week) and camera operator (requiring two to four hours per week). To discuss the possibilities available at KAID-TV, contact the Outreach Director at the number given.

> **KAID-TV**
> 1910 University Drive
> Boise, ID 83725
> Tel: 208-373-7316

KVUE-TV

Internship

If you're serious about working in the television broadcasting industry, this internship at KVUE-TV in Austin is certainly appealing. Interns at KVUE-TV are treated like employees and are expected to conduct themselves accordingly. In order to be considered, you must have a lot of self-discipline. You're expected to work independently and get the assigned work done in the allotted amount of time. KVUE-TV only accepts students who are earning high school credit for the internship. The number of hours you work a week is based on the number of credits you're earning and the requirements of your school. KVUE-TV usually takes one or two high school students a year. However, the station accepts up to fifteen college interns first, and high school students are accepted only if there's room. Internships usually follow the school calendar. To apply for an internship, contact the station directly.

> **KVUE-TV**
> PO Box 9927
> Austin, TX 78766
> Tel: 512-459-9442
> Email: sedillo@kvue.com

MediaOne

Field Experience, Volunteer Opportunity

MediaOne offers a unique job shadowing program for high school students interested in TV broadcasting. The amount of time you spend shadowing any one job is flexible, and the longer you stay, the more you get to experience. Some students spend only one day at the station, just to glimpse the world of professional broadcasting. Others might come one day a week for several months to take a deeper look at the field. You usually shadow one specific job, such as that of producer, for example. Eventually, if you stick with it, you could get to operate a camera, help produce a show or two, or handle some of the audio and visual controls. MediaOne usually takes eight students per semester to shadow, and schools rarely issue credit for such voluntary, sporadic work. Shadowing is set up only through teachers and career counselors, so talk to your counselor if you're interested in arranging some shadowing at MediaOne. Your counselor can contact the station directly to discuss all the possibilities of the voluntary shadow program.

■ **MediaOne**
688 Industrial Drive
Elmhurst, IL 60126
Tel: 630-717-2407

THE MUSEUM OF TELEVISION AND RADIO
Internship

If you're especially interested in the history of television and radio, this could be the opportunity you've been looking for. The Museum of Television and Radio, with locations in New York City and Los Angeles, offers internships to high school students. Although there's not a formal program, the museums are happy to accept highly motivated students who possess a keen interest in the radio and television industry. You must have an eye for detail, some computer training, and the ability to work well with others. Interns often develop their own project or help the museum in a particular area in need of research. Internships are designed to meet the needs of individuals and their schools. How many hours you'll put in each week, and whether or not you'll receive high school credit, is something to work out with your career counselor. Most students work at the museum about eight hours a week for one semester. Full-year internships are also possible. School-to-work and work-study students are welcome. Interns commute to the museums, and no residential facilities are available.

To intern at the Los Angeles museum, call the museum directly to discuss your interests and schedule. If you live in New York City, you must write the museum a formal letter of intention, describing in detail your interests and what kind of internship you propose; phone calls are not accepted. The museum's Web site is good for general information, but information about high school internships is not available there.

■ **The Museum of Television and Radio**
Los Angeles Branch: 465 North Beverly Drive
Beverly Hills, CA 90210
Tel: 310-786-1034
Email: cfantozzi@mtr.org
Web: http://www.mtr.org
New York City Branch: 25 West 52nd Street
New York, NY 10019
Attn: Internship Program

Summer Scholars Program
College Course/Summer Study

Washington and Lee University, which created the nation's very first journalism program back in the 1860s, now offers a mass media journalism course for rising seniors in its Summer Scholars Program. Participants in this residential program spend four weeks in July studying all aspects of today's mass media: legal and ethical issues, writing and marketing, as well as a general history. In the program, you spend three hours each weekday in class and visit both a major newspaper and a TV station. You and your classmates are also responsible for running a student newspaper and operating a campus FM radio station. Only twenty students are accepted into the journalism course each year so, while the competition is strong, you benefit from more individualized attention. There is time to take advantage of the fine computer, library, and athletic facilities at Washington and Lee University, and to participate in group excursions and activities on the weekends. Applicants must submit a form, standardized test results, and the recommendation of a teacher or counselor by mid-May. Program fees, including room and board, total about $1,700; textbooks, travel, and personal expenses are extra. Financial aid is available to those who demonstrate need as well as high academic standing. For further details and an application form, contact the Director of Summer Scholars.

■ **Summer Scholars Program**
Washington and Lee University
Office of Special Programs
Lexington, VA 24450-0303
Tel: 540-463-8723

Syracuse University Summer College Programs
College Course/Summer Study

Syracuse University offers students interested in broadcasting the opportunity to explore the field via its Summer College Programs. Those who have completed their sophomore, junior, or senior year of high school are eligible to apply to the Summer College, which runs for six weeks from late June to early

August. Broadcasting is just one part of the Public Communications Program, in which students also study advertising, journalism, and public relations. The Public Communications Program centers on the "Communications and Society" course—the foundation course for all of Syracuse's undergraduate degree programs in communications—and field trips and activities related to that course. You also take another college-level course in any liberal arts subject you choose. Upon satisfactory completion of the courses, you receive credit from Syracuse University.

Summer College is not just about academics, but also about adapting to the university environment and experiencing campus life. Residential participants live in campus dormitories, use on-campus recreational and educational facilities, and work and live with university faculty and students. Tuition is about $2,500, while room and board is an additional $1,000. Books and supplies may cost an extra $75 to $150. Some financial aid is available, and should be requested when applying for admission. A completed application form, letter of recommendation from a school official, and a current transcript must be submitted to the Summer College by early June (those applying for financial aid should submit materials by early May). Contact Syracuse University Summer College Programs for an application and for more details.

■ **Syracuse University Summer College Programs**
309 Lyman Hall
Syracuse, NY 13244-1270
Tel: 315-443-5297

Tech Trek Summer Camp at KTEH-TV
Camp

KTEH-TV, public television for San Jose, sponsors the Tech Trek Summer Camp in conjunction with the Educational Media Center (ITV) of the Santa Clara County Office of Education. Students ages twelve to seventeen are welcome to attend the camp, which provides an introduction to broadcasting careers and technology. There are two identical Tech Trek sessions, one in mid-July and one in early August; each lasts for one week. During that time, students produce, shoot, and edit their own videos under the direction of production professionals. Contact KTEH-TV for further details, including location and pricing information. It is best to inquire early, as each session can accommodate only twenty students.

Tech Trek Summer Camp at KTEH-TV
1585 Schallenberger Road
San Jose, CA 95131
Tel: 408-795-5451

TELEVISION INSTITUTE

College Course/Summer Study

Wright State University (WSU) offers a wide variety of residential precollege programs every July for high school students. If you are a rising junior or senior considering a career in television, WSU has an interesting study option for you. The Television Institute is one week of instruction and exploration of the broadcasting field right in the university's own television studio. All participants work in small groups to produce their own programs, undertaking all the necessary roles from camera operator to floor director to on-screen talent. It is a busy week, but you also have time to explore the Wright State University campus and to experience being away at college. Only twenty-four spaces are available in the Television Institute, so early submission of your application form and letter of recommendation is recommended. The all-inclusive cost for the program is about $500. WSU awards college credit to all those who successfully complete the program. For further details, contact the Office of Precollege Programs.

Television Institute
Wright State University
Office of Precollege Programs
163 Millett Hall
3640 Colonel Glenn Highway
Dayton, OH 45435-0001
Tel: 937-775-3135

UNIVERSITY OF NORTH CAROLINA CENTER FOR PUBLIC TELEVISION

Field Experience, Volunteer Opportunity

UNC's Center for Public Television offers high school volunteers the chance to shadow professionals on the job. The center usually takes two or three students a year to work at UNCTV, a public broadcasting station, and shadow certain broadcasting positions. Usually, you job shadow a few hours a week. To job shadow at the Center for Public Television, your school career counselor must make the initial contact. To find out more about UNCTV, visit its Web site.

University of North Carolina Center for Public Television
PO Box 12231
Research Triangle Park, NC 27709-4900
Tel: 919-549-7077
Web: http://www.unctv.org

Waccamaw Media

Internship

Waccamaw Media usually takes two local high school students each semester to intern at their production studio. Their program is very structured, and you work ten hours a week with the production manager doing specific jobs. You edit tapes, use the camera, and do voice-overs and dubbing. As an intern, you get to do shoots for two of Waccamaw's productions. One, *Country Images,* is a local spot filmed on location in Myrtle Beach, South Carolina. The other, *Nascar Dash Races,* features twenty-six races a year, and Maccamaw Media covers them all. Myrtle Beach is the home of the Career Center for Radio and Television, a vocational school for high school students. Students attending the Career Center often come to Waccamaw Media to intern, but all students are welcome to apply to the program. You must work through your high school career counselor to develop an internship plan and schedule that works for you. Schools often give high school credit for internships at Waccamaw Media. Acceptance into the program is based on a personal interview.

- **Waccamaw Media**
  350 Wesley, Suite 102
  Myrtle Beach, SC 29577
  Tel: 803-236-8188
  Web: http://www.waccmedia.com
  Email: jblood@sccoast.net

WKMS-FM

Internship

WKMS-FM offers internships to high school students who are eager to learn about all the aspects of operating a public radio station. Interested students must demonstrate a good academic performance and be referred by a teacher. Once accepted into a position with the station, interns have a range of duties in the areas of operations, archives, and programming. Contact WKMS-FM for further details on the application process and position availabilities.

- **WKMS-FM**
  2018 University Station
  Murray, KY 42071

WNVC-TV

Internship

WNVC-TV is a public television station broadcasting programs from around the world to the diverse population of the Washington, DC, area. It welcomes high school students to apply for the many internships it has available. Maturity and willingness to learn are more important than age, but preference is often given to college undergraduates. A programming intern is needed to assist the programming director in contacting international distributors, testing the marketplace, and liaising with foreign program producers. WNVC-TV also uses a public relations intern to write press releases and correspond with the international community in Washington, among other duties. You also may choose to apply to be a marketing intern, working with the marketing director to find corporate support for the station, or to be a development intern, helping the membership director retain members and coordinate volunteers. Finally, there is the possibility of serving as a management intern, who provides administrative support to the station's general manager. All of these internship positions require a commitment of between ten and fifteen hours per week, and usually last one semester. Apply several weeks in advance to the Internship Coordinator.

■ **WNVC-TV**
8101A Lee Highway
Falls Church, VA 22042
Tel: 703-698-9682

Do It Yourself

First

"What are you going to do after high school?" How many times have you heard that question? If you haven't heard it yet, you will . . . and for a while it may seem like you hear it every five minutes. You might try these replies to shock and appall your neighbors and relatives: A) "I'm not finishing high school." B) "I'm supposed to do something after high school?" C) "Spend all my time writing poetry for my Web page" or D) "I'm going into broadcasting." Okay . . . most people won't be appalled that you want to pursue a career in broadcasting, but they probably will realize just how tough it can be to get a job in radio and television. Broadcast journalism schools are being criticized for sending graduates out into the world unprepared for the intense competition for the limited number of jobs. Ownership of radio stations is frequently changing hands, resulting in lost jobs or combined positions. News departments can't afford to hire all the reporters they need, so there are always many applicants for the few available job openings and internships. And if you want to direct, produce, or write for the major networks and cable stations, your road to success is even rockier. But enough of the doom and gloom—for the ambitious, talented, well-trained, and well-educated student of broadcasting, there are many great opportunities and potential career paths. And if you start pursuing your career while still in high school, you'll be well ahead of the game.

Once you decide to answer the world's questions with choice D—"I'm going into broadcasting"—you're likely to be met with even more questions. The creative side or the technical side? Will you work in the news division or the entertainment division? Will you work on-camera or off-camera? People will ask these questions because if there's one industry everybody knows about, it's the TV and radio industry. Maybe you have a good answer already. Perhaps you've been passionate about the weather since you were a kid, standing in the middle of storms, watching the movement of ominous clouds and performing rain dances. "I'll be a TV meteorologist," you say. Or maybe you've been active in sports ever since you could first lift a baseball bat, and see sports announcing in your future. Or perhaps you had a Close 'n Play record player as a little kid and drove your family crazy by spinning Mom's Olivia Newton-John 45s day and night—you're a future radio disc jockey if there ever was one. For many people, careers in radio and TV speak to lifelong passions. So why not get started as early as you can? When people start asking you, "What are you going to do *after* high school?" wouldn't it be great to tell them what you're doing now, while you're still *in* high school?

Even in the smallest towns, there are extracurricular activities that can help you develop valuable experience—school newspapers, yearbooks, and drama and media clubs. You probably even have better opportunities than high school students of ten years ago; now, many high schools are running their own radio stations and TV video departments. And if none of these clubs and departments exist in your school? That's even better—you'll have the chance to be a pioneer in your school, setting up new programs and gaining hands-on experience.

LeAlan Jones and Lloyd Newman are two high school students who recently drew national attention to their work—attention which led to the creation of a brand new journalism award for students. Following the murder of a five-year-old boy in the housing project in which LeAlan lived, LeAlan and Lloyd taped interviews with the victim's family and neighbors. They also interviewed the families of the two boys who committed the murder. The resulting report won the national Robert F. Kennedy Journalism Award, beating out hundreds of entries from professional journalists across the country. Channel One News (a news program with reports produced by students) and the Robert F. Kennedy Memorial then created a contest for student reporting in print and broadcast news.

Such credentials and efforts will undoubtedly help LeAlan and Lloyd in whatever careers they pursue, but you don't have to win national awards and inspire the creation of new scholarships to gain the attention of employers and internship directors. Even small-scale efforts can help you along your chosen career path: volunteering at a local public television station; doing the radio play-by-play for your high school sporting events; videotaping school programs; writing, directing, and producing your own play for a drama club.

Broadcast Journalism in School

One of the easiest ways to get started in broadcasting may already exist in your own school: TV clubs and radio stations are popping up in high schools all over the country. Students are producing and directing their own programming, as well as learning how to operate cameras and other necessary equipment. For example, a high school in Dearborn, Michigan, has involved students in a video club for several years now, and alumni of the program have gone on to direct films, produce television series, and other high profile careers in the industry.

If your school doesn't currently have such a program, try to get one started. Ask a journalism or English teacher, or any interested faculty member, for help and guidance. Research other high school broadcasting departments. Visit any local radio and TV stations, and see what instructional and financial help they can offer. Price video and other equipment, and come up with a complete proposal outlining expenses, staff requirements, and the educational benefits to the students. You may not actually see the final results while still in high school—such programs can take years to develop. But you'll still be able to learn a lot about broadcasting in the process.

It's true that your school simply may not be able to offer radio and TV clubs or classes due to the expense of broadcasting equipment or a lack of widespread interest. But virtually every high school has a school newspaper and yearbook, and you should seriously consider getting involved with the publications at your school. As a member of the staff, you will develop writing skills, which can be your most important asset in broadcasting work. You'll also develop interviewing skills and be required to keep up with current events, politics, and cultural trends.

Theater and Drama

Ever get in trouble for being the class clown? Your teachers may revise their criticism when you go on to great success as the writer for a network sitcom. Okay, that might be a long, difficult journey—or you may enjoy overnight success. That's the nature of the entertainment business—it's totally unpredictable. But if you're ready to take on the fierce competition of writing, directing, or producing for television dramas, comedies, and made-for-TV movies, there are ways to prepare while still in high school.

Just as some people are passionate about news and sports, others are passionate about performing and the arts. It's this passion that can help see the young writer/producer/director through the lean times. Without this passion, you may be better off becoming a doctor or a lawyer—something with security. But somebody has to create all the hundreds of episodes of soap operas, sitcoms, prime-time dramas, and other entertainment programs that air every year, so it might as well be you!

Your high school drama department can give you a taste of what goes into producing a show on a small scale. Most schools put much funding into sports programs (or even video and radio programs), leaving theater programs to struggle on their own. Actually, this creates a great chance for you to get actively involved in a production from beginning to end. You can get funding for a production by contacting local businesses for donations, or selling them ads to be placed in a play bill. Promotion can also be a big part of a radio and TV producer's job, and every high school theater department requires volunteers to publicize a production.

Your high school theater department probably offers great opportunities to young technicians interested in learning about production equipment. Lighting, sound, and set design are very important to the success of a stage play. As part of the technical crew, you'll probably also use camera, editing, and other video equipment to record the play.

You may think the drama club is only for actors, but it may give you the chance to write and direct your own plays as well. If not, propose a "junior" program to your drama club advisor—such a program can give high school students a chance to direct junior high or grade school students in original plays. Collaborate on a full-length play with other writers you know, or write your own one-act. Four or five student one-acts can make for a two-hour production, giving many student writers and directors the chance to cast their own plays, direct, and see their own projects performed for an audience.

In small towns, community theaters can always use volunteers for their productions. Or start your own community theater; the playwright and director Sam Shepard honed his writing and directing skills by staging a different production every week in his own apartment.

Speech teams are often associated with high school theater departments. Whether your area of interest is news, radio, or entertainment, a speech team can help you develop speaking and writing skills. Such skills are very important to radio disc jockeys, news anchors, broadcast meteorologists, and sportscasters.

And don't forget about your community radio station; some stations are pleased to help talented young writers and performers produce original programs. Submit a script and proposal for a radio show, along with a tape of your work. When taping a radio show, you'll learn a lot about how a radio show is produced, and how a station is managed. Though the majority of radio stations today offer music-only formats, public radio stations broadcast variety shows, musical concerts, documentaries, and talk shows. Garrison Keillor started his "Prairie Home Companion" music and comedy program at Minnesota Public Radio; it is now broadcast nationally, and has spawned several books, audio recordings, and even a catalog company.

INTERNING AND VOLUNTEERING

Though some high school students interested in writing, directing, and producing have their sights set high on national network jobs, others want to work in smaller cities and less stressful environments. Fortunately, many cities across the country have at least one network-affiliated TV station, and there are over 1,500 radio stations operating in the United States. This means plenty of job opportunities for people wanting to work outside of California, New York, and Washington, DC. It can also mean opportunities for you to learn about the industry while still in high school.

A simple way to begin exploring the radio and television industry—indeed, almost any industry—is to shadow a professional. Some schools have shadowing programs that can introduce you to a professional who will answer your questions and allow you to experience a typical day at the studio. If there is no formal program in place, perhaps a journalism teacher or guidance counselor can help you get in touch with a pro. Or ask your parents and your friends' parents if they have any contacts in the broadcasting industry. Make the effort to find a shadowing opportunity because it will show you the reality of the industry like nothing else can. Shadowing will help you make well-informed career decisions. And, if you get along well with the professional you shadow, it may lead to a volunteer, intern, or part-time position.

Volunteering and interning are crucial to securing employment in radio and television because experience counts in this competitive industry. Local stations may not have formal internship programs or they may only offer internships to college students; this is where your persistence can pay off. (Well, "pay off" in learning opportunities, not cash; you'll more than likely be working for free!) Let resistant station managers know how ambitious you are by getting to know them and making sure they know you. Send them a resume with a list of your high school achievements, extra-curricular activities, and course work. Include a cover letter that spells out exactly what kind of work you are willing to do (anything!) and when you are available (anytime outside of the school day!) Call news producers and other professionals to check with them about creating an internship position. And don't give up! Some stations initially may not be interested in training a high school student, but your determination might change a few minds.

If an internship just isn't a possibility, try to arrange a less formal position. Volunteer to come in whenever they need your help, perhaps with filing or mass mailing. Public television and radio stations frequently need volunteers to help with fundraising and even production. While cataloguing videotapes or sorting mail is probably not your ultimate career goal, voluntarily performing such tasks clearly displays your commitment and dedication to the field. This kind of work can also help you make contacts that will prove useful when you've graduated from college and are looking for a job.

Conclusion

Because there's so much competition for every broadcasting job available, the sooner you can get started pursuing your interests, the more experience you can gain. Your high school and your community probably already offer many programs in which you can participate. But remember—don't be discouraged if there don't seem to be many chances to learn about broadcasting in your town. You can create your own chances by getting to know local professionals and other students who share your interests. Such efforts and persistence will lead you in the direction of a great future.

Surf the Web

First

You must use the Internet to do research, to find out, to explore. The Internet is the closest you'll get to what's happening now all around the world. This chapter gets you started with an annotated list of Web sites related to broadcasting. Try a few. Follow the links. Maybe even venture as far as asking questions in a chat room. The more you read about and interact with those in the field of broadcasting, the better prepared you'll be when you're old enough to participate as a professional.

One caveat: you probably already know that URLs change all the time. If a Web address listed below is out of date, try searching on the site's name or other key words. Chances are, if it's still out there, you'll find it. If it's not, maybe you'll find something better!

The List

Broadcast Employment Services
http://www.tvjobs.com/index_a.htm

If you're looking for information about finding a job in television broadcasting, you'll find it here. This site is great for job seekers, but it also provides solid information and resources for students who are just considering the field. The site is divided into the broad areas of Employment, Reference, Education, Networking, and Miscellaneous. In the Networking section, there's a place to connect with other students to talk about your career pursuits. The Education section is another good place to visit. A list of internships includes offerings by television stations, cable stations, broadcasting groups, and production studios across the United States. Another useful feature in the Education section is a list of broadcasting schools and colleges. Under Employment, you'll find bulletin boards, job banks, and job lines, all packed with available positions. This is a great place to sneak a peek at other people's resumes to get ideas. If you're looking for advice from professionals, be sure to spend some time at the recently added NetForum section. Here, you can browse through topics of discussion, ask questions, and receive responses from those working in the field.

Broadcasters Training Network
http://www.learn-by-doing.com/

If you're unsure about how to get started as a broadcaster, this site might be just the thing, since its tag line is "the most effective way to begin a career in radio broadcasting." The core of the Broadcasters Training Network (BTN) is an apprenticeship program at local radio stations for students fresh out of high school. The program matches each student with an instructor already working at the station. For instance, if you want to become a disk jockey or a sports broadcaster, you'll work with someone who's currently performing that job in your area. This site thoroughly explains how the program works, complete with testimonials. The careers described in greatest detail are disc jockey, news reporter, talk show host, sportscaster, and production engineer. Apprentices pay a hefty placement fee for the program, which lasts four to six months. The philosophy of BTN is that your money and time are better spent on this intensive training program than on a liberal arts diploma. That's something you can evaluate for yourself by comparing BTN's fee to other training options, such as paid internships, volunteering, or a college degree.

Careers in Broadcasting
http://www.snybuf.edu/~cdc/sidebarframe.htm

This site was created by a career development center at Buffalo State College in New York. It is all text, but it gives a nice overview of numerous low- and high-profile jobs in broadcasting, including camera operator, media coordinator, news writer, programming director, sportscaster, video/audio technician, and at least a dozen more. Under each category of employment, you'll find a description of general job responsibilities and common job titles, plus tips on college courses that will help you qualify for the position. Throughout this site, you'll discover little nuggets of wisdom. For instance, did you know that production assistant jobs are the most common entry point for broadcasting majors and are in extremely high demand? Another paragraph points out that not all broadcasting jobs are found in radio and TV stations, and that there are opportunities with production companies, advertising agencies, and other audio/video organizations. You'll also learn that radio jobs are usually easier to find than television jobs, and that spending time at a small station can prepare you well for work in a larger market. Finally, there's a long list of books that might be useful.

Electronic Field Trip to Kentucky Educational Television
http://www.ket.org/Trips/KET/High.html

The point of this site is to familiarize middle and high school students with a variety of television broadcast careers. It gives information on the skills and educational requirements for each job, plus links to colleges and universities with broadcast degree programs. The field trip is broken into three main sections: pre-production, production, and post-production jobs. Under each section, you'll see a list of job titles, many of which overlap from one section to the next. You click on the specific career—say, broadcast engineer—to learn that this title is further divided into the jobs of video engineer, videotape engineer, and maintenance engineer. For each job, there are brief entries about general responsibilities, kinds of equipment used, job skills required, and typical salaries. One big complaint about this site is its dizzying use of multiple frames, sacrificing the readability of a single large frame. Moreover, you'll feel like you're constantly clicking, only to arrive at a frame that requires you to click again to get just a bit more information. If you start getting frustrated with this site, maybe the solution is to take a real field trip to your local TV station.

ESPN SportsZone
http://ESPN.SportsZone.com/

When it comes to sportscasting, ESPN is head and shoulders above the competition—on the Web as well as on TV. This site covers baseball, football, hockey, soccer, golf, basketball, auto racing, tennis, and more. It is arranged in a dynamic, easy-to-navigate style, with up-to-the-minute headlines filling up two-thirds of the home page. A column on the left-hand side of the page lists each sport ESPN covers in detail, as well as other areas like interactive polls, fantasy sports, and health and fitness. Once you're finished checking the latest scores, click on ESPN Studios for actual career-related information. At the time of review, ESPN Studios was hiring freelancers to input statistical data on sporting events. You can even fill out and send an application on-line. In addition, you'll want to spend some time reviewing the career trajectories of the current on-air talent. Just go to the Personalities section, where you'll find bios of over one hundred popular sportscasters.

Fall River Educational Television
http://www.fallriver.mec.edu/tvfred/tvfred.htm

This site will fill you in on the ambitious television broadcasting work that's being done by students of B.M.C. Durfee High School and other schools in Fall River, Massachusetts. Students are actively involved in the planning, maintenance, production, editing, and airing of a variety of programming on a local channel. What's really unique is the extensive television production curriculum in the high school. The TV1 class gives students the basics and theory of television production. They learn one-camera remote setup, as well as the importance of lighting and audio in producing a quality program. TV2 exposes students to studio tapings and "taped as live" shows. In TV3, students work on "highly produced" television production. The final project is to produce a senior video yearbook. If these classes seem like something your school could reasonably offer, tell your principal about this site.

Internet Screenwriters Network
http://www.screenwriters.com/hn/writing/screennet.html

Here's an interesting site for both aspiring and working screenwriters. On your first visit, be sure to stop by the Screenwriters Lounge to rub electronic elbows with professionals. Along with advice on breaking into the field, you'll find detailed analyses of several film scripts here. These will get you thinking about screenplays like a writer does—considering the choices made in point of view, the power of a strong opening, and the decision to show or to tell important information. In another area, called Columns, Newsletters & Special Features, you'll find all of the above. One regular column here is "Breaking In." It's penned by a script consultant and gives you the dirt on writing and revising your first screenplay. The section called "Do's and Don'ts for Writers" covers everything from writing a query letter to good phone etiquette. "Movie Reviews for Writers" offers a breakdown of the movie's story structure in each review. To be an official member, you need to have sold at least one screenplay, but even as a nonmember you'll have access to almost all the areas of this site.

The National Association of Broadcasters
http://www.nab.org/

If you're a junkie for all things related to broadcasting, this is a site you'll have to visit. The A-Z index of the site's contents is an excellent way to find specific topics, such as children's television or the Telecommunications Act of 1996. The site, however, was designed for someone working in the industry, and you may find some of the topics too esoteric for a fledgling broadcaster. For instance, you probably won't be drawn to the sections that focus on government, legal/regulations, and science/technology as they relate to broadcasting. However, you'll find an extremely useful link in the membership section. It's to the site for the Broadcast Education Association (http://www.usu.edu/~bea), the arm of NAB that reaches out to a student audience. The Broadcast Education Association's mission is to prepare students for jobs in the industry and provide useful information for professors as well. Elsewhere at this site, you can read about past and future BEA conventions, where students are often active participants and speakers.

Peterson's Guide to Summer Programs for Teenagers
http://www.petersons.com/summerop/

Finding a camp that suits your interests is easy enough at this site—just search Peterson's database of academic, travel, and camping programs. Type in the keyword "broadcasting," for instance, and you'll bring up a list of links to a number of summer programs, including the Washington Summer Seminars in Media, New York University Tisch School of the Arts, and World Horizons International. Then click on a specific program or camp for a quick overview description. In some instances, you'll get a more in-depth description, along with photographs, applications, and on-line brochures. If you need to limit your search to your home state, that's easy enough too. You can sift through Peterson's database by geographic region or alphabetically.

RadioSpace
http://www.radiospace.com

If you're working at your school's radio station, you're probably operating on a shoestring budget. RadioSpace could be a great resource for you. It's a radio broadcasting agency that provides news and programming services to radio stations, thanks to the assistance of corporations, government agencies, and nonprofit organizations. Choose from headlines under the topics of business and technology, consumer, current events, entertainment, health, or personal finance. Radio stations can download (for free) the fully produced report in a choice of formats, or read through the written transcript to use portions of the story. For example, the National Institutes of Health Radio News Service developed a story about a new treatment that prevents strokes in children with sickle cell anemia. Another story, provided by *U.S. News & World Report,* focused on a bill President Clinton was going to sign that day. If you're putting together your own story, RadioSpace also provides the Consumer Experts Directory of people from various companies and organizations willing to be interviewed on topics ranging from alternative fuel sources to debt management. You'll also find a link to the *Yearbook of Experts, Authorities, and Spokespersons,* an encyclopedia of sources used by journalists. And click on Cool Radio Resources if you want to locate everything from a site on early American radio to one stocked with nifty sound effects.

RADIO-TELEVISION NEWS DIRECTORS ASSOCIATION (RTNDA)
http://www.rtnda.org/

This Web site is hosted by an organization that serves electronic journalists in more than thirty countries. While very little of this site is aimed directly at students, once you dip into the text, you'll find plenty to absorb. Start by reading RTNDA's on-line *Communicator* magazine, which offers in-depth features on the impact of technology on electronic journalism, the role electronic journalism plays in politics and public policy, and cultural diversity in the field, among other topics. Look for valuable information about scholarship programs under a section called "Membership Benefits." RTNDA annually awards thirteen undergraduate and graduate scholarships, all of which include an all-expenses-paid trip to the organization's international conference. There is also an internship program that's part of the Newsroom Diversity Campaign in which a number of three- and six-month paid internships are awarded to minority journalism students to learn and receive hands-on experience in news management at radio and television stations across the country.

THE SCREENWRITER'S NOTEBOOK
http://www.a1.com/derringer/scrnwrtr.html

The home page of the Screenwriter's Notebook may not be very exciting, but don't judge this book by its drab cover. This site can lead you to many other good sites and save you a lot of on-line searching. For instance, click on the section called "Nuts and Bolts" to link to a bevy of sites that cover the craft of screenwriting. In the "Voices of Experience" section, choose from a number of sites where working screenwriters share their mistakes and successes. The "Reference Shelf" section provides an on-line library where you can conduct research to strengthen the factual accuracy of your script. You can also click on links that will tell you about screenwriters' workshops, seminars, and conferences. Finally, be sure to visit "Recommended Reading" to view a list of excellent books on screenwriting (plus comments about each book so you can pick and choose the ones worth tracking down).

Sweeps 2000
http://www.geocities.com/Hollywood/Hills/4741/

This site might offer some inspiration if your high school studies are in need of some excitement. Sweeps 2000 is an interdisciplinary project in television/multimedia production for students at West Orange High School in Winter Garden, Florida. Television production is used as a focal point for a number of other subjects such as earth science, English, global studies, math, technology, and speech. All student work culminates in Sweeps Week, in which each class produces a news broadcast that is judged and graded. The earth science class, for example, tracks the weather and makes its own weather predictions using tools on the Internet. These predictions are presented in three-minute television reports. In the English class, students work on script writing and reading. Their final project is graded on the script's original content and how well it is presented on camera. This site goes into tremendous detail, making it easy to use as a blueprint at your own school. For example, each subject area contains listings called "Digging Deeper" and "Teacher Follow-up" that point you and your teachers to additional sources of information.

Television and Radio News Research
http://www.missouri.edu/~jourvs/

A professor at the renowned Missouri School of Journalism created this site in order to offer a behind-the-scenes glimpse at television and news broadcasting. He has conducted a number of national surveys on topics such as newsroom profitability, salaries, staff diversity, and the use of interns. The text looks honestly at some of the less glamorous aspects of the industry. For instance, one chapter studies how broadcast news salaries have kept up with inflation. Another chapter considers the insufficiency of staff benefits at American TV and radio stations. Yet another examines how minorities and women have fared in the TV news work force in the 1990s. You'll definitely want to click on "Pros and Cons of Broadcast Careers," a lengthy, well-written article that can help you decide whether this is the right career path for you. Here, you can compare your personality traits and career values to the survey of people who are working in the field.

Tripod
http://www.tripod.com/work/internships/

Tripod is a magazine-style Web site that focuses on four broad topics: Work, Money, Living, and Health. You'll want to beeline toward the Work pages, where you can search the latest edition of the *National Directory of Internships*, which was created by the National Society of Experiential Education. It works like this: you conduct your search by picking a career category from a long list, then selecting a geographic region. For instance, a search for internships related to broadcasting anywhere in the United States netted some with the Center for Media Education, Discovery Communications, and several large radio and TV stations. You could also search under categories like "film and video production" or "journalism." Or you can just search by keywords. For example, type in "television" or "production" and up comes a list of potential internships. You'll have to spend about two minutes signing up as an official member, then another five minutes waiting for an email that reveals your secret member password. But what's seven minutes when you're looking for the internship that'll launch your career?

WeatherNet
http://cirrus.sprl.umich.edu/wxnet/

The WeatherNet site—which claims to be the Internet's premier source of weather information—is tailor-made for the aspiring weatherperson. If you are considering a career in weather reporting, the only thing that might alarm you about this site is that it could put you out of a job someday. Even the casual weather watcher can't help but be impressed by FastForecast, in which you input your zip code to get current local weather conditions (and the moon phase to boot). The WeatherCams are another cool feature. These provide live, daily photos of weather conditions in more than 120 cities around North America. There's also a library of weather software that you can download to track hurricanes, create severe weather maps, and pursue other weather-related research. Should you have any time left, choose from several newsgroups for weather enthusiasts and chat away. Finally, if there just isn't enough for you at this exhaustive site, perhaps you'll want to follow the links to nearly three hundred additional weather sites.

Read a Book

First

When it comes to finding out about radio and television, don't overlook a book. (You're reading one now, after all.) What follows is a short, annotated list of books and periodicals related to radio and television. The books range from fiction to personal accounts of what it's like to be a director to professional volumes on specific topics, such as TV commercials. Don't be afraid to check out the professional journals, either. The technical stuff may be way above your head right now, but if you take the time to become familiar with one or two, you're bound to pick up some of what is important to radio and television personnel, not to mention begin to feel like a part of their world, which is what you're interested in, right?

We've tried to include recent materials as well as old favorites. Always check for the latest editions, and, if you find an author you like, ask your librarian to help you find more. Keep reading good books!

Books

Ball, William. *A Sense of Direction: Some Observations on the Art of Directing.* Candid, personal account of his methods in the art and craft of directing by a master in the field. While most of Ball's experience was in the theater, his skill in the director's process from first reading through final production is applicable to television work as well. New York: Drama Book Publishers, 1984.

Berland, Terry and Deborah Ouelette. *Breaking into Commercials: The Complete Guide to Marketing Yourself, Auditioning to Win, and Getting the Job.* An inside look at the TV industry and commercial acting written jointly by a woman who runs a casting company and an award-winning photographer/writer. New York: Penguin, 1997.

Blumenthal, Howard. *Careers in Television: You Can Do It!* Describes careers behind the scenes and in front of the camera with twenty different perspectives on the television industry. Boston: Little, Brown, 1992.

Boyd, Andrew. *Broadcast Journalism: Techniques of Radio and TV News.* Updated manual for would-be journalists in radio and TV, including news gathering, writing, interviewing, recording, and editing. Boston: Focal Press, 1997.

Carter, Bill. *The Late Shift: Letterman, Leno, and the Network Battle for the Night.* Gripping account of the backstage intrigue set off by Johnny Carson's announcement that he would retire from late night television. New York: Hyperion, 1995.

Cooper, Donna. *Writing Great Screenplays for Film and TV: Learn the Art and Craft of Screenwriting from a Top Instructor at the AFI Film School.* 2nd edition. Associated with such hit series as "ER" and "Law and Order," Cooper gives top level advice from her screenwriting classes at the school of the American Film Institute. New York: Arco, 1997.

Cowgill, Linda J. *Writing Short Films: Structure and Content for Screenwriters.* An acclaimed screenwriter and teacher in various film schools, Cowgill cites numerous examples from films short and long to stress strategies for keeping your script on track, developing strong characters, and using compelling writing. Los Angeles: Lone Eagle, 1997.

Donald, Anabel. *The Glass Ceiling.* Third in a series of mysteries about a fictional television researcher and part-time private eye. In this story Alex Tanner is in a race against time to keep her anonymous client from murdering four famous feminists. New York: St. Martin's Press, 1994.

Dougan, Pat. *Professional Acting in Television Commercials: Techniques, Exercises, Copy, and Storyboards.* A comprehensive guide by an actress, teacher, trainer, and director who has herself appeared in over 650 commercials, TV shows, and stage plays. Portsmouth, NH: Heinemann, 1995.

Dunne, John Gregory. *Monster: Living Off the Big Screen.* A mordantly funny insider's look at working in Hollywood and getting your scripts written, bought, and produced. New York: Random House, 1997.

Engel, Joel. *Screenwriters on Screenwriting: The Best in the Business Discuss Their Craft.* Using a question-and-answer format, many of the finest screenwriters in the film and TV business discuss the tricks of their trade. A fine guide to the realities of the business as well as tips for creating the best screenplays. New York: Hyperion, 1995.

England, Gary. *Weathering the Storm: Tornadoes, Television and Turmoil.* A veteran weathercaster describes his career, which paralleled many of the changes and advances in the science of meteorology. Norman, OK: University of Oklahoma Press, 1996.

Field, Shelly. *100 Best Careers in Entertainment.* A comprehensive guide for those entering the entertainment business. Covers job facts, qualifications, employment opportunities, and descriptive information on a wide variety of careers in the radio, television, stage, and recordings industries. New York: Macmillan, 1995.

Fiske, John. *Television Culture.* A comprehensive introduction for students in communication and media studies courses, this book offers a thorough study of the cultural processes that underlie television's development and narrative forms. London: Routledge, 1991.

Henson, Robert. *Television Weathercasting: A History.* Covers both the lighthearted and serious aspects of television weather, including changes in the style of reporting over the years and profiles of celebrities who began their careers in weathercasting. Jefferson, NC: McFarland & Co., 1990.

Kanner, Ellie and Paul G. Bens, Jr. *NEXT! An Actor's Guide to Auditioning.* Two of Hollywood's top casting directors give a complete analysis of the auditioning process with strategies and techniques for knowing what a casting director is looking for and increasing your chances for getting the part you want. Los Angeles: Lone Eagle, 1997.

Katz, Jon. *Sign Off.* A novel for the 1990s involving the ruthless takeover of a once-great TV network and its most respected division, USB News. The author, a former executive producer for CBS Morning News, now teaches journalism at New York University and writes for media publications. New York: Bantam, 1991.

Kisseloff, Jeff. *The Box: An Oral History of Television 1920-1961.* A fascinating look at the beginnings of television, from the pioneering inventor Philo Farnsworth through the news, comedy, and drama creators in the early days of the medium. Intertwined throughout a chronological narrative are 300 interviews with those involved in the business, technological, and entertainment sides of the industry. New York: Penguin, 1995.

Listfield, Emily. *The Last Good Night: A Novel.* A television anchorwoman's shadowy past catches up with her in this riveting novel of psychological suspense. Boston: Little, Brown, 1997.

Looker, Thomas. *The Sound and the Story: NPR and the Art of Radio.* A background look at National Public Radio by a radio veteran from the all night staff of "Morning Edition." Looker asserts that radio prompts listeners to see and respond to the world around them with greater insight, depth, and compassion. Boston: Houghton Mifflin, 1995.

Lutgens, Frederick K. and Edward J. Tarbuck. *The Atmosphere: An Introduction to Meteorology.* 7th Edition. This introductory text to the field of weather forecasting gives an in-depth treatment that is accessible to the beginner in the field. Enhanced with full color photographs, maps, and charts. New York: Prentice-Hall, 1997.

Maltin, Leonard. *The Great American Broadcast: A Celebration of Radio's Golden Age.* One of America's leading authorities on film, and an ardent radio buff, gives a factual history of the beginning of radio through its heyday to the bittersweet end of an era. Based on hundreds of personal interviews and behind-the-scenes stories from actors, directors, writers, producers, and sound-effects wizards. New York: Dutton, 1997.

Marc, David and Robert J. Thompson. *Prime Time, Prime Movers: From I Love Lucy to L.A. Law—America's Greatest TV Shows and the People Who Created Them.* Learn about the backgrounds and professional styles of top performers, producers, and writers in the history of television. Highly readable and informative. Syracuse, NY: Syracuse University Press, 1995.

Millerson, Gerald. *Effective TV Production.* 3rd Edition. A thorough overview of the production process that outlines the main functions of every job in the industry and indicates how they are interrelated. Other books by Millerson on lighting, scenic design, and camera techniques are considered among the best in the field. Oxford: Focal Press, 1993.

Nisbett, Alec. *The Sound Studio.* A textbook for audio engineers, directors, writers, performers, and students, with the emphasis on general principles and understanding the importance of each operation and innovation in sound recording. Boston: Focal Press, 1995.

Postman, Neil and Steve Powers. *How to Watch TV News.* A professor and a TV journalist discuss the difference between what television news says it is presenting and what it actually delivers. They ask a provocative question: Are we becoming a less knowledgeable nation because of the entertainment aspect of television news? New York: Penguin, 1992.

Resnik, Gail and Scott Trost. *All You Need to Know about the Movie and TV Business.* Two prominent entertainment attorneys guide the novice through the treacherous waters of the profession, including a breakdown of job descriptions, contracts, deal-making, and copyright law. New York: Simon & Schuster, 1996.

Stamberg, Susan. *Talk!: NPR's Susan Stamberg Considers All Things.* "Story-gathering was my joyful habit before it became a career. Working as a broadcaster lets me turn an impulse into a profession." Interviews and vignettes from the award-winning commentator's distinguished career in public radio. New York: Random House, 1993.

Thomas, Dave with Robert Crane and Susan Carney. *SCTV: Behind the Scenes.* Members of the Second City stage company, which transformed itself into an innovative late-night TV show, present anecdotes and interviews with producers, comedians, and backstage workers about their highly successful television experience. Toronto: McClellend and Stewart, 1997.

Walter, Richard. *The Whole Picture: Strategies for Screenwriting Success in the New Hollywood.* Professor and chair of the UCLA Film and Television Writing Program, Walter has mentored a generation of screenwriters. He explores the full spectrum of essential skills needed in this field. New York: Penguin, 1997.

PERIODICALS

Broadcasting and Cable: The News Weekly of Television and Radio. Weekly. A major trade publication for anyone affiliated with the TV, radio, or cable broadcasting fields. Includes Nielsen ratings, job listings, personality profiles, advertising, and marketing. 1705 DeSales St., NW, Washington, DC 20036. 202-659-2340. http://www.broadcastingcable.com

Cablevision: The Analysis and Features Bi-Weekly of the Cable Television Industry. Bi-Weekly. Of interest to those engaged in every aspect of the cable television industry. Covers technology operations, programming, marketing, and pay-per-view with specific columns on customer service and policy-making. 825 Seventh Ave., New York, NY 10019. 212-887-8400.

Communicator: The Magazine for Electronic Journalists. Monthly. Official journal of the Radio-Television News Directors Association that covers issues in news gathering, management, and production for major networks as well as local broadcasting stations throughout the country. RTNDA, 1000 Connecticut Ave., NW, Suite 615, Washington, DC 20036. 202-659-6510. http://www.rtnda.org

Current. Bi-weekly. A journal for and about people involved in public radio and public television, from producers to station employees. Interviews, programming, and news items on PBS and NPR, plus a classified section posting jobs in public broadcasting. 1612 K St., NW, Suite 704, Washington, DC 20006. 202-463-7055.

Electronic Media: The Programming Publication. Weekly. All the latest news in the fast-changing world of electronic media, cable communications, and digital broadcasting. Includes classified ads for jobs in producing, engineering, reporting, and editing throughout the country. 740 N. Rush St., Chicago, IL 60611-2590. 312-649-5200. http://www.emonline.com

Emmy. Bi-monthly. Published for members of the Academy of Television Arts and Sciences, this journal will interest general readers with close-ups of people in the news and articles on trends and topics in the world of television. 5220 Lankersheim Blvd., North Hollywood, CA 91601-3107. 818-754-2800.

Journal of Broadcasting and Electronic Media. Quarterly. Treatment of the media in this journal covers all aspects of how media affects the social sciences. Each article is preceded by an abstract, making it easy to browse. 1771 N St., NW, Washington, DC 10036. 202-429-5354.

Journal of Popular Film and Television. Scholarly title that emphasizes U.S. popular film with a socio-cultural analysis of film theory and criticism. 1319 Eighteenth St., NW, Washington, DC 20036-1802. 202-296-6267.

Mediaweek: The News Magazine of the Media. Weekly. All aspects of network television, cable, radio, and magazine publishing are included in this information-packed journal in personality profiles, news items, job listings, and analysis articles. 1515 Broadway, New York, NY 10036. 212-536-5336.

Popular Communications. Monthly. Articles cover radio history and nostalgia, amateur radio, VHF scanners, short-wave receivers, and antenna technology. Monitors virtually all aspects of communications technology. 76 N. Broadway, Hicksville, NY 11801-2953. 516-681-2922.

Satellite TV Week. Weekly. Covers satellite TV programming with articles on personalities, industry news, sports coverage, and channel listings. 140 S. Fortuna Blvd., Fortuna, CA 95540-0308. 707-725-6951.

Television Quarterly. Quarterly. This publication of the National Academy of Television Arts and Sciences focuses on articles that "discuss the social, political, economic, and technological issues of the medium." 111 W. 57th St., New York, NY 10019. 212-586-8424.

Videomaker. Monthly. Written for beginners and professional technicians with an emphasis on camcorders, desktop video, copywriting, animation software, reviews, and much more. Intended for those using video in hobbies, business, or education. Box 4591, Chico, CA 95927. 916-891-8410.

Ask for Money

First

By the time most students get around to thinking about applying for scholarships, they have already extolled their personal and academic virtues to such lengths in essays and interviews for college applications that even their own grandmothers wouldn't recognize them. The thought of filling out yet another application form fills students with dread. And why bother? Won't the same five or six kids who have been fighting over grade point averages since the fifth grade walk away with all the really *good* scholarships?

The truth is, most of the scholarships available to high school and college students are being offered because an organization wants to promote interest in a particular field, encourage more students to become qualified to enter it, and finally, to help those students afford an education. Certainly, having a good grade point average is a valuable asset, and many organizations who grant scholarships request that only applicants with a minimum grade point average apply. More often than not, however, grade point averages aren't even mentioned; the focus is on the area of interest and what a student has done to distinguish himself or herself in that area. In fact, frequently the *only* requirement is that the scholarship applicant must be studying in a particular area.

Guidelines

When applying for scholarships there are a few simple guidelines that can help ease the process considerably.

Plan Ahead

The absolute worst thing you can do is wait until the last minute. For one thing, obtaining recommendations or other supporting data in time to meet an application deadline is incredibly difficult. For another, no one does their best thinking or writing under the gun. So get off to a good start by reviewing scholarship applications as early as possible—months, even a year, in advance. If the current scholarship information isn't available, ask for a copy of last year's version. Once you have the scholarship information or application in hand, give it a thorough read. Try and determine how your experience or situation best fits into the scholarship, or even if it fits at all.

If possible, research the award or scholarship, including past recipients and, where applicable, the person in whose name the scholarship is offered. Often, scholarships are established to memorialize an individual who majored in religious studies or loved history, but in other cases, the scholarship memorializes the *work* of an individual. In those cases, try and get a feel for the spirit of the person's work. If you have any similar interests or experiences, don't hesitate to mention these.

Talk to others who received the scholarship, or to students currently studying in the same area or field of interest in which the scholarship is offered, and try to gain insight into possible applications or work related to that field. When you're working on the essay asking why you want this scholarship, you'll have real answers: "I would benefit from receiving this scholarship because studying engineering will help me to design inexpensive but attractive and structurally sound urban housing."

Take your time writing the essays. Make certain you are answering the question or questions on the application and not merely restating facts about yourself. Don't be afraid to get creative; try to imagine what you would think of if you had to sift through hundreds of applications. What would you want to know about the candidate? What would convince you that someone was deserving of the scholarship? Work through several drafts and have someone whose advice you respect—a parent, teacher, or guidance counselor—review the essay for grammar and content.

Finally, if you know in advance which scholarships you want to apply for, there might still be time to stack the deck in your favor by getting an internship, volunteering, or working part-time. Bottom line: the more you know about a scholarship and the sooner you learn it, the better.

Follow Directions
Think of it this way—many of the organizations who offer scholarships devote 99.9 percent of their time to something other than the scholarship for which you are applying. Don't make a nuisance of yourself by pestering them for information. Follow the directions on applications and supporting materials. If the scholarship materials specify that you write for further information, write for it—don't call.

Pay close attention to whether you're applying for an award, a scholarship, a prize, or other financial aid. These words are often used interchangeably, but just as often they have different meanings. An award is usually given for something you have done: built a park or helped distribute meals to the elderly; or something you have created: a design; an essay; a short film; a screenplay; an invention. On the other hand, a scholarship is frequently a renewable sum of money that is given to a person to help defray the costs of college. Scholarships are given to candidates who meet the necessary criterion based on essays, eligibility, grades, or a combination of the three.

Supply all the necessary documents, information, and fees and make the deadlines. You won't win any scholarships by forgetting to include a recommendation from your history teacher or failing to postmark the application by the deadline. Bottom line: get it right the first time, on time.

Apply Early
Once you have the application in hand, don't dawdle. If you've requested it far enough in advance, there shouldn't be any reason for you not to turn it well in advance of the deadline. You never know, if it comes down to two candidates, your timeliness just might be the deciding factor. Bottom line: don't wait, don't hesitate.

Be Yourself
Don't make promises you can't keep. There are plenty of hefty scholarships available, but if they require you to study something that you don't enjoy, you'll be miserable in college. And the side effects from switching majors after you've accepted a scholarship could be even worse. Bottom line: be yourself.

Don't Limit Yourself
There are many sources for scholarships, beginning with your guidance counselor and ending with the Internet. All of the search engines have education categories. Start there and search by keywords, such as "financial aid," "scholarship," "award." Don't be limited to the scholarships listed in these pages.

If you know of an organization related to or involved with the field of your choice, write a letter asking if they offer scholarships. If they don't offer scholarships, don't let that stop you. Write them another letter, or better yet, schedule a meeting with the president or someone in the public relations office and ask them if they would be willing to sponsor a scholarship for you. Of course, you'll need to prepare yourself well for such a meeting because you're selling a priceless commodity—yourself. Don't be shy, be confident. Tell them all about yourself, what you want to study and why, and let them know what you would be willing to do in exchange—volunteer at their favorite charity, write up reports on your progress in school, or work part-time on school breaks, full-time during the summer. Explain why you're a wise investment. Bottom line: the sky's the limit.

THE LIST

Academy of Motion Pictures Arts and Sciences (AMPAS)
8949 Wilshire Boulevard
Beverly Hills, CA 90211-1972
Tel: 310-247-3000

AMPAS sponsors the Student Academy Awards and Nichol Screenwritng Award.

Ben Chatfield Scholarship
Radio and Television News Directors Foundation
1000 Connecticut Avenue, NW, Suite 615
Washington, DC 20036
Tel: 202-659-6510

Eligible are sophomore or more advanced undergraduate students enrolled in electronic journalism in a college or university where such a major is offered. Applications must include one to three examples of reporting or producing skills on audio or video cassette tapes (no more than fifteen minutes total), a statement explaining why the candidate seeks a career in broadcast or cable journalism, and a letter of endorsement from a faculty sponsor that includes a description of available facilities for electronic news production. This scholarship is for $1,000, paid in semi-annual installments of $500.

Broadcast Pioneers Scholarship
Broadcast Education Association
1771 N Street, NW
Washington, DC 20036-2891
Tel: 202-429-5354

College juniors, seniors, and graduate students in any area of broadcasting are eligible. Two awards worth an average of $1,250 are given each year.

Bruce Dennis Scholarship
Radio and Television News Directors Foundation
1000 Connecticut Avenue, NW, Suite 615
Washington, DC 20036
Tel: 202-659-6510

Eligible are sophomores or more advanced undergraduate students enrolled in electronic journalism in a college or university where such a major is offered. Applications must include one to three examples of reporting or producing skills on audio or video cassette tapes (no more than fifteen minutes total), a statement explaining why the candidate seeks a career in broadcast or cable journalism, and a letter of endorsement from a faculty sponsor that includes a description of available facilities for electronic news production. This scholarship is $1,000, paid in semi-annual installments of $500.

Bruce Palmer Scholarship
Radio and Television News Directors Foundation
1000 Connecticut Avenue, NW, Suite 615
Washington, DC 20036
Tel: 202- 659-6510

Eligible are sophomore or more advanced undergraduate students enrolled in electronic journalism in a college or university where such a major is offered. Applications must include one to three examples of reporting or producing skills on audio or video cassette tapes (no more than fifteen minutes total), a statement explaining why the candidate seeks a career in broadcast or cable journalism, and a letter of endorsement from a faculty sponsor that includes a description of available facilities for electronic news production. This scholarship is $1,000, paid in semi-annual installments of $500 each.

Chicago Association of Black Journalists Scholarships
PO Box 11425
Chicago, IL 60611
Tel: 312-409-9392

Applicants must be Native American, Eskimo, Asian-American, African-American or Hispanic; enrolled at a four-year institution; studying in Illinois; and have an interest in photography, photogrammetry, filmmaking, or writing. Eight awards ranging from $1,000 to $2,500 are given each year.

College Television Awards
Academy of Television Arts and Sciences
5220 Lankershim Boulevard
North Hollywood, CA 91601
Tel: 818-754-2800

The College Television Awards competition rewards excellence in college student film/video productions honoring student producers. All entries must have been made for college course credit between September 1 and December 15 to qualify. Entries longer than one hour will not be accepted. News, sports, and magazine shows and comedy entries must not exceed thirty minutes. Entries must be submitted on 3/4" videotape only.

Edward R. Murrow Awards
Radio and Television News Directors Foundation
1000 Connecticut Avenue, NW, Suite 615
Washington, DC 20036
Tel: 202-659-6510

The awards recognize excellence in electronic journalism. Categories: spot news, features reporting, series documentary, investigative reporting, sports reporting, sound or video, and newscast. There are eight awards given every year.

Elaine Noll Scholarship
Texas Professional Communicators
PO Box 173
Denison, TX 75020

Applicants must be enrolled in a two- or four-year institution, female, and studying in Texas. One award worth $1,000 is given each year.

Environmental and Scientific Reporting Fellowship
Radio and Television News Directors Foundation
1000 Connecticut Avenue, NW, Suite 615
Washington, DC 20036
Tel: 202-659-6510

Must be employed in electronic news with fewer than three years full-time experience and demonstrated excellence in environmental reporting.

Goldwater Scholarship
American Radio Relay League Foundation
225 Main Street
Newington, CT 06111
Tel: 860-666-1541

American Radio Relay League Foundation offers a scholarship for $5,000 for a licensed radio amateur majoring in communications.

Graham Foundation/Sigma Delta Chi Scholarships
Sigma Delta Chi Foundation of Washington
9206 Bulls Run Parkway
Bethesda, MD 20817-8430
Tel: 301-530-8430

Applicant must be a full-time sophomore or junior with a credible scholastic record, demonstrated financial need, and a commitment to go into journalism as a career. Applicant must submit six examples of accomplishments in journalism and the name of a professor or institutional faculty member who will provide a letter or endorsement under separate cover. Finalists will be called for an interview. There are ten awards available to students at schools in the Washington metro area: five from Sigma Delta Chi and five from Gridiron Foundation.

Harold E. Ennes Scholarship Fund
Society of Broadcast Engineers
8445 Keystone Crossing, Suite 140
Indianapolis, IN 46240
Tel: 317-253-1640

Applicants must have a career interest in the technical aspects of broadcasting and be recommended by two members of the Society of Broadcast Engineers. Preference will be given to members of SBE. The two awards vary between $500 and $1,000.

Harold E. Fellows Memorial Scholarship
National Association of Broadcasters
1771 N Street, NW
Washington, DC 20036-2891
Tel: 202-429-5380

The applicant or his/her parent must have worked for a broadcasting station affiliated with the National Association of Broadcasters. Four awards worth an average of $1,250 each are presented each year.

Jacque Minotte Health Reporting Scholarship
Radio and Television News Directors Foundation
1000 Connecticut Avenue, NW, Suite 615
Washington, DC 20036
Tel: 202-659-6510

To a promising young reporter who wants to cover health or medical stories, one award worth $1,000 is given each year.

James Lawrence Fly Scholarship
Broadcast Education Association
1771 N Street, NW
Washington, DC 20036-2891
Tel: 202-429-5354

This scholarship of $2,500 is awarded based on superior academic performance and potential. Applicants must attend schools with at least one Broadcast Education Association member.

Kaltenborn Foundation Grant
349 Seaview Avenue
Palm Beach, FL 33480
Tel: 305-655-8024

The grants are for scholarly studies in the field of written communications, including projects concerned with television, radio, the press, and magazines. Include some background biographical information as well as one or two references with your project proposal. Grants are given for written studies which might be suitable for publication, not for loans or general tuition fees.

Len Allen Award of Merit
Radio and Television News Directors Foundation
1000 Connecticut Avenue, NW, Suite 615
Washington, DC 20036
Tel: 202-659-6510

To recognize and reward an outstanding student whose career objective is radio news or news management. Eligible are sophomore or more advanced undergraduate or graduate students enrolled in an electronic journalism sequence at an accredited or nationally recognized college or university. Applications must include one to three examples of reporting or producing skills on audio or video cassette tapes (no more than fifteen minutes total), a statement explaining why the candidate seeks a career in broadcast or cable journalism, and a letter of endorsement from a faculty sponsor that includes a description of available facilities for electronic news production. The scholarship is $1,000, paid in semi-annual installments of $500 each. An expense-paid trip to the Radio and Television News Directors Association Annual International Convention is also provided.

■ National Association of Black Journalists
Box 17212
Washington, DC 20041
Tel: 703-684-1270

Applicants must have selected as a career either journalism or communications, be under eighteen years of age, and be African-American. Two awards of $2,500 each are given each year.

■ National Association of Broadcasters
Broadcasting Research and Information Group
1771 N Street, NW
Washington, DC 20036-2891
Tel: 202-429-5380

Applicants must be entering senior year in college and must submit a proposal. The average award is $5,000.

■ Radio and Television News Directors Foundation Fellowship
1000 Connecticut Avenue, NW, Suite 615
Washington, DC 20036-3690
Tel: 202-659-6510

There are nine awards of $1,000 given every year.

■ Richard "Dick" Cheverton Scholarship
Radio and Television News Directors Foundation
1000 Connecticut Avenue, NW, Suite 615
Washington, DC 20036
Tel: 202-659-6510

Eligible are sophomores or more advanced undergraduate students enrolled in electronic journalism in a college or university where such a major is offered. Applications must include one to three examples of reporting or producing skills on audio or video cassette tapes (no more than fifteen minutes total), a statement explaining why the candidate seeks a career in broadcast or cable journalism, and a letter of endorsement from a faculty sponsor that includes a description of available facilities for electronic news production. This scholarship is $1,000, paid in semi-annual installments of $500.

■ Scripps Howard Foundation Scholarships
1100 Central Trust Tower
PO Box 5380
Cincinnati, OH 45201
Tel: 513-977-3055

Available to undergraduates and graduate students with continuing interest and work in the field of journalism, or in graphic arts as applied to the newspaper industry, residing in or attending schools located in communities served by Scripps Howard operations. Qualified students should submit a typewritten mailing label, with the words "scholarship application" and their name and home mailing address by December 20. Application packets will be mailed in late December, which are to be completed and returned by February 25. Evidence of work in the field of journalism or graphic arts, such as high school or college newspapers, magazines, radio or television stations, or in private industry should be submitted with the scholarship application. Applicants must be US citizens in financial need. The award amount varies between $500 and $3,000.

■ Shane Media Scholarship
Broadcast Education Association
1771 N Street, NW
Washington, DC 20036-2891
Tel: 202-429-5354

Applicants must be juniors, seniors, or graduate students enrolled in full-time degree work at a college or university where at least one department is an institutional member of the Broadcast Education Association. Selection is based on evidence that the applicant possesses high integrity, superior academic ability, potential to be an outstanding radio professional, and a well-articulated sense of personal and professional responsibility. The stipend is $3,000.

■ Theodore "Ted" Koop Scholarship
Radio and Television News Directors Foundation
1000 Connecticut Avenue, NW, Suite 615
Washington, DC 20036
Tel: 202-659-6510

To provide financial assistance for the undergraduate education of a student whose career objective is radio or television news. Eligible are sophomore or more advanced undergraduate students enrolled in electronic journalism in a college or university where such a major is offered. Applications must include one to three examples of reporting or producing skills on audio or video cassette tapes (no more than fifteen minutes total), a statement explaining why the candidate seeks a career in broadcast or cable journalism, and a letter of endorsement from a faculty sponsor that includes a description of available facilities for electronic news production. This scholarship is $1,000, paid in semi-annual installments of $500.

Vincent Wasilewski Scholarship
Broadcast Education Association
1771 N Street, NW
Washington, DC 20036-2891
Tel: 202-429-5354

Must be at least a sophomore attending a school with a BEA member. Awards are based on superior academic performance and potential. The amount of each award and the number of awards vary each year.

Walter Patterson Scholarship
National Association of Broadcasters
1771 N Street, NW
Washington, DC 20036-2891
Tel: 202-429-5380

For study toward a career in broadcasting. There are two awards of $1,250 given every year.

Look to the Pros

FIRST

The following professional organizations offer a variety of materials, from career brochures to lists of accredited schools to salary surveys. Many of them also publish journals and newsletters that you should become familiar with. Some also have annual conferences that you might be able to attend. (While you may not be able to attend a conference as a participant, it may be possible to "cover" one for your school or even your local paper, especially if your school has a related club.)

When contacting professional organizations, keep in mind that they all exist primarily to serve their members, be it through continuing education, professional licensure, political lobbying, or just "keeping up with the profession." While many are strongly interested in promoting their profession and passing information about it to the general public, these busy professional organizations are not there solely to provide you with information. Whether you call or write, be courteous, brief, and to the point. Know what you need and ask for it. If the organization has a Web site, check it out first: what you're looking for may be available there for downloading, or you may find a list of prices or instructions, such as sending a self-addressed stamped envelope with your request. Finally, be aware that organizations, like people, move. To save time when writing, first confirm the address, preferably with a quick phone call to the organization itself, "Hello, I'm calling to confirm your address...."

The Sources

■ **The Accrediting Council on Education in Journalism and Mass Communications**
Stauffer/Flint Hall
University of Kansas
Lawrence, KS 66045
Tel: 913-864-3986
Web: http://www.ukans.edu/~acejmc

Contact ACEJMC for information about schools.

■ **American Meteorological Society (AMS)**
45 Beacon Street
Boston, MA 02108
617-227-2425
Web: http://www.ametsoc.org/AMS/amsedu/index.html

Contact AMS for information on their education programs, scholarships, summer opportunities and related programs.

■ **American Women in Radio and Television**
1650 Tysons Boulevard, Suite 200
McLean, VA 22102
703-506-3290
Web: http://www.awrt.org

Contact AWRT for information on careers in radio and television, as well as scholarships and internships.

■ **Association of Independent Television Stations**
1320 19th Street, NW, Suite 300
Washington, DC 20036
Tel: 202-887-1970

Contact AITS for information on their summer internship.

■ **Broadcast Education Association**
1771 N Street, NW
Washington, DC 20036-2891
Tel: 202-429-5354
Web: http://www.beaweb/org

An association of university broadcasting faculty, BEA offers annual scholarships in broadcasting for college juniors, seniors, and graduate students.

Broadcast Employment Services
http://www.tvjobs.com

BES is an on-line service providing job listings, employment-wanted notices, and information on scholarships, internships, and careers in television broadcasting.

Corporation for Public Broadcasting
Publications
901 E Street, NW
Washington, DC 20004-2037
Tel: 202-879-9600
Web: http://www.cpb.org/

CPB offers *Careers in Public Broadcasting,* 12 pages, which describes careers in the field and cites minority job banks and minority media professional organizations. CPB also publishes a *Guide to Volunteer and Internship Programs in Public Broadcasting.*

ESPN, Inc.
Human Resources Department
935 Middle Street
Bristol, CT 06010
Tel: 860-585-2000
Web: http://espn.sportszone.com/editors/studios/

ESPN has a recorded job line and information on internships for college seniors.

National Association of Broadcasters
1771 N Street, NW
Washington, DC 20036-2891
Tel: 202-429-5355
Web: http://www.nab.org/

Contact NAB for a catalog of their publications on broadcasting.

Producers Guild of America
400 South Beverly Drive, Suite 211
Beverly Hills, CA 90212
Tel: 310-557-0807

Contact PGA for general information about television production.

■ Radio-Television News Directors Association
1000 Connecticut Avenue, NW, Suite 615
Washington, DC 20036
202-659-6510
Web: http://www.rtnda.org/

Contact RTNDA for *Careers in Radio and Television News*, $5, 24 pages, which discusses qualifications, responsibilities, and how to prepare yourself and get a job. RTNDA also offers scholarship and internship information.

■ Society of Broadcast Engineers, Inc.
8445 Keystone Crossing, Suite 140
Indianapolis, IN 46240
317-253-1640
Web: http://www.sbe.org/

Contact SBE for information on their many professional publications.

■ Society of Motion Picture and Television Engineers
595 West Hartsdale Avenue
White Plains, NY 10607
Tel: 914-761-1100
Web: http://www.smpte.org

Several publications are available on career opportunities for engineers in television, film, and the production and postproduction fields. Contact the society or visit the Web site for a current list of publications.

■ The Society of Professional Journalists
16 South Jackson Street
Greencastle, IN 46135
Tel: 765-653-3333
Web: http://spj.org

Contact the SPJ for information on student chapters, scholarships, educational information, and much more.

Index

A

ABC, 5, 6
Academy of Motion Pictures Arts and Sciences (AMPAS), 154
Academy of Television Arts and Sciences, College Television Awards, 155-156
Accrediting Council on Education in Journalism and Mass Communications (ACEJMC), 55, 164
Actors, 13
Actresses, 13
Advanced Television Test Center (ATTC), 115-116
Agents, 60
Allen, Len, Award of Merit, 158-159
American Collegiate Adventures (ACA), 116
American Federation of Television and Radio Artists (AFTRA), 36, 55
American Meteorological Society (AMS), 102, 103, 164
American Women in Radio and Television, 164
Anchors. See Radio anchors; Television anchors
Animators, 10
Announcer. See Correspondents; Disc jockeys; Radio anchors; Radio producers; Reporters; Television anchors
Apollo 13, 5
Association of Independent Television Stations, 164

B

Berra, Lawrence "Yogi," 71
Best boy, 11
Books, 143-147
Brinkley, David, 15
Broadcast Education Association, 164
Broadcast Employment Services, 165
    website for, 135-136
Broadcast engineer, 11, 19-28
Broadcasters Training Network website, 136
Broadcasting Training Program, 15
Broadcast journalist. See Correspondents; Reporters
Broadcast meteorologist. See Weather forecaster
Broadcast operator. See Broadcast engineer
Broadcast Pioneers Scholarship, 154
Broadcast technician, 19. See also Broadcast engineer
Buck's Rock Camp, 116-117

C

Cable television networks, 7
Camp Chi, 117-118
Camps, 110
Careers in Broadcasting website, 136-137
Cartoonists, 10
Casting agents, 10
CBS, 5, 6
Challenger explosion, 5
Chatfield, Ben, Scholarship, 154
Cheverton, Richard "Dick," Scholarship, 159-160
Chicago Association of Black Journalists Scholarships, 155
Chief engineers, 11-12, 21, 26
Chief meteorologists, 103
College courses/summer study, 110
Columbia College Chicago, High School Summer Institute, 120-121
Comedians, 13
Community affairs directors, 12
Continuity writers, 10
Cornell University Summer College, 119
Corporation for Public Broadcasting, 120, 165
Correspondents, 10, 13, 49-58
Costume designers, 10

167

D

d'Aquino, Iva, 4
Dennis, Bruce, Scholarship, 155
DGA-Walt Disney TV Directors Training Program, 83-84
Diana, Princess, 5
Director. See Television director
Directors Guild of America, 83, 84
Directors of photography, 11
Disc jockeys, 10-11, 13, 29-38
DJ. See Disc jockeys
Documentary writer, 62

E

Eagle Communications (KECI-TV, KTVM-TV), 120
Electrical technicians, 11
Electronic Field Trip to Kentucky Educational Television website, 137
Engineers, 11-12
Ennes, Harold E., Scholarship Fund, 157
Environmental and Scientific Reporting Fellowship, 156
ESPN, Inc., 165
  website for, 137-138
Executive producer. See Television producer

F

Fall River Educational Television website, 138
Federal Communications Commission (FCC), 5, 7-8, 25
Federal Radio Commission, 7-8
Fellows, Harold E., Memorial Scholarship, 157
Fessenden, Reginald A., 4
Field experience, 111
Field technicians, 20. See also Broadcast engineer
Film directors, 85
Film writers, 66
Floor manager, 11

Fly, James Lawrence, Scholarship, 158
Foreign correspondents, 56
FOX, 5, 6
Freed, Alan, 31
The Freedom Bureau, 58

G

Gaffers, 11
General managers, 9, 74, 85, 94, 103
General sales managers, 36
Gillars, Mildred, 4
Godfrey, Arthur, 31
Goldwater Scholarship, 156-157
Graham Foundation/Sigma Delta Chi Scholarships, 157
Graphic artists, 10
Grip, 11

H

Hairstylists, 10
Hauptmann, Bruno, 7
HBO, 7
Herrold, Sybil, 31
Hindenberg explosion, 53

I

Institute on Political Journalism, 93
International Brotherhood of Electrical Workers, 25
International Radio and Television Society, 121
Internet Screenwriters Network website, 138
Internships, 111

J

Jack, Wolfman, 31

K

KAID-TV, 122

Kaltenborn Foundation Grant, 158
Kennedy, John F., 5
Koop, Theodore "Ted," Scholarship, 160-161
KVUE-TV, 122

L

Letterman, David, 101
Lighting directors, 11
Lindbergh, Charles, 7
"The Love Boat," 7

M

Maintenance technicians, 20. See also Broadcast engineer
Makeup artists, 10
Management, 9
Manitou-Wabing Sports and Arts Center, 118-119
Marconi, Guglielmo, 4
Marketing workers, 12
"M*A*S*H," 7
MediOne, 122-123
Minorities in Broadcasting Training Program, 55
Minotte, Jacque, Health Reporting Scholarship, 158
Morrison, Herb, 53
Murrow, Edward R., Awards, 156
Museum of Television and Radio, 123-124
Music librarians, 10

N

Narrowcasting, 15
National Association of Black Journalists, 159
National Association of Broadcast Employees and Technicians AFL-CIO (NABET), 25
National Association of Broadcasters (NAB), 15, 27, 46, 159, 165
  website for, 139

Index

National Broadcasting Company (NBC), 4, 5, 7
National Center for Environmental Prediction, 100
National Hurricane Center, 100
National Weather Association (NWA), 102, 103
National Weather Service, 100
News anchors, 40-41, 56, 74, 85, 94, 103. See also Correspondents; Reporters
Newscaster. See Radio anchors; Television anchors
News directors, 46, 94
Newsperson. See Radio anchors; Television anchors
Newswriters, 10
Noll, Elaine, Scholarship, 156
North Carolina, University of, Center for Public Television, 126

O

Off-air careers, 9-12
On-air careers, 12-13
On-air personality. See Disc jockeys; Radio producers
Oswald, Lee Harvey, 5

P

Palmer, Bruce, Scholarship, 155
Patterson, Walter, Scholarship, 161
PBS, 5
Periodicals, 147-149
Peterson's Guide to Summer Programs for Teenagers website, 139
Play-by-play announcer. See Sportscaster
Postproduction, 9
Preproduction, 9
Press secretaries, 46
Producers, 26, 46, 66, 74, 85. See also Television producer
Producers Guild of America, 165
Production, 9

Professional organizations, 163-166
Program assistants, 11
Program directors, 9. See also Disc jockeys; Radio producers
Promotion manager, 12
Props workers, 10

R

Radio anchors, 13, 39-48
Radio and Television News Directors Foundation
  Ben Chatfield Scholarship, 154
  Bruce Dennis Scholarship, 155
  Bruce Palmer Scholarship, 155
  Edward R. Murrow Awards, 156
  Environmental and Scientific Reporting Fellowship, 156
  Jacque Minotte Health Reporting Scholarship, 158
  Len Allen Award of Merit, 158-159
  Richard "Dick" Cheverton Scholarship, 159-160
  Theodore "Ted" Koop Scholarship, 160-161
Radio and Television News Directors Foundation Fellowship, 159
Radio commentators, 13
Radio producers, 10-11, 13, 29-38
Radio reporters, 13
RadioSpace website, 139-140
Radio-Television News Directors Association (RTNDA), 47, 83, 166
  website for, 140
Reagan, Ronald, 14
Reporters, 10, 49-58
Roosevelt, Franklin D., 4, 5
Ruby, Jack, 5

S

Sales manager, 12
Salespeople, 12
Scenic designers, 10
Scheduling assistant, 21
Scholarships, 151-161

Screenwriters, 10, 59-68
The Screenwriter's Notebook website, 140-141
Scripps Howard Foundation Scholarships, 160
Scriptwriter. See Screenwriter
Severe Storms Forecast Center, 100
Shane Media Scholarship, 160
Showtime, 7
Sigma Delta Chi Foundation of Washington, Graham Foundation/Sigma Delta Chi Scholarships, 157
Simpson, O. J., trial of, 7
Society of Broadcast Engineers, Inc., 24, 27, 166
  Harold E. Ennes Scholarship Fund, 157
Society of Motion Picture and Television Engineers, 166
Society of Professional Journalists, 55, 58, 166
Sports anchor, 40. See also Sportscaster
Sportscasters, 13, 69-86
Sports director. See Sportscaster
Staff writer. See Screenwriter
Station managers, 36, 56
Storm Prediction Center, 100
Story editor. See Screenwriter
Stuntpeople, 13
Sweeps 2000 website, 141
Syracuse University Summer College Programs, 124-125

T

Talk show hosts, 13
Technical directors, 26
Technical stock clerks, 20
Tech Trek Summer Camp at KTEH-TV, 125-126
Television anchors, 13, 39-48
Television and Radio News Research website, 141-142
Television commentators, 13

169

Television directors, 11, 66, 77-86
Television producers, 10, 87-96
Television reporters, 13
Texas Professional Communicators, Elaine Noll Scholarship, 156
Traffic department, 9
Traffic manager, 9
Transmitter engineers, 11
Tripod website, 142
TV news anchors, 36

U

UPN, 5

V

Video control technician. See Broadcast engineer
Video director, 12
Video editors, 12
Videographers, 28
Video recording technicians, 20-21
Video-robo technician, 20. *See also Broadcast engineer*
Video technicians, 20. *See also Broadcast engineer*
Vietnam War, 5
Volunteer opportunities, 112

W

Waccamaw Media, 127
Wade, Lawrence, Journalism Fellowship, 93
Washington and Lee University, Summer Scholars Program, 124
Wasilewski, Vincent, Scholarship, 161
WB, 5
Weathercaster. See Weather forecaster
Weather forecaster, 13, 97-106
WeatherNet website, 142
Weather reporter. See Weather forecaster
Web sites, 135-142
Welles, Orson, 4
WKMS-FM, 127
WNVC-TV, 127-128
World Wide Web, 5
Wright State University, Television Institute, 126
Writer/producer. See Television producer
Writers Guild of America (WGA), 66

X

"The X-Files," 7